Praise for *Honest to God*

If you are tired of the game and are searching for something more authentic, then you have to read Josh's call to a more honest and transparent walk with God. With a compellingly articulated combination of present day stories and biblical reflections from the lives of those whose hearts chased after God, Josh has charted a course for those of us who want to be honest with God.

—DR. JOE STOWELL
President, Cornerstone University

We love our masks—those elaborate covers of self-protection constructed daily in hopes of concealing our wounds, our doubts, and our brokenness. Thankfully, God calls us out, inviting us into His light, where all things—even wounds, doubts, and brokenness—will be made new. In a culture hungry for authenticity, Weidmann's book is a profound exploration of biblical authenticity. It's an amplification of God's glorious invitation to acknowledge who we really are, and so uncover more of who we're being made to be.

—MIKE YANKOSKI
Author of *Under the Overpass*

With a deeply pastoral heart, Weidmann dares you to be honest. Showing how honesty is at the heart of true growth, and digging into all the ways we seek to hide and cover, he casts a vision for true authenticity in the midst of grace.

—KYLE STROBEL, PhD
Author and Cofounder of Metamorpha

Drawing on Josh's own faith journey, *Honest to God* calls a new generation to crave transparency with God, face our own people-games, and address the fallout that can result. Identifying struggles such as image management, Josh helps the reader with practical "how to" steps. What I found most refreshing was his exploration of our times of anger with God. Young people who want a serious discussion have found it.

—ANDREW J. SCHMUTZER, PhD
Professor of Biblical Studies, Moody Bible Institute and author of *The Long Journey Home: Understanding and Ministering to the Sexually Abused*

In his book *Honest to God*, Josh urges us to drop whatever masks we might be wearing and dare to be real with God. He models that kind of honesty by sharing of his own faults and shortcomings. As the apostle Paul said, "If I must boast, I will boast of the things that show my weakness" (2 Corinthians 11:30). *Honest to God* is a gospel-centered book that will speak not only to youth, but to anyone who is struggling with people-pleasing tendencies or hypocrisy. In other words, it speaks to all of us.

—**DAVID JONES**
Senior Pastor, Village Church of Barrington

Josh Weidmann offers the gift of freedom in Christ with a fresh perspective, written powerfully and woven with self-disclosing humor, from the precious heart of a pastor. In *Honest to God*, we are provided with the opportunity to exhale and breathe in the truth before us: Living honestly before God fulfills our own desire to choose life and live fully every day.

—**MAUREEN YOCKEY**
Executive Director, Alternatives Pregnancy Center

Josh Weidmann wants to live, and Jesus came to make us alive! *Honest to God* offers the first steps of authenticity on the way to the glorious kingdom where grace, truth, and love are the invitation to become sons and daughters of our Father.

—**WES YODER**
Author of *Bond of Brothers: Connecting with Other Men Beyond Work, Weather and Sports*

Josh Weidmann's book *Honest to God* reveals a life-transforming truth, that when you are truly honest to God, it is IMPOSSIBLE to stay the same! God already knows it all, so why not lay it bare before Him? This book has caused me to re-evaluate my approach before God.

—**MIKE ROMBERGER**
Senior Pastor, Mission Hills Church

Not only is Josh Weidmann a world-class evangelist, but also a passionate writer and a born storyteller who spurs his readers to greater depths of devotion and commitment to God. In *Honest to God*, he combines biblical, personal, and pastoral insight with a desperately needed message of transformation through honesty.

—**BENIAMIN PASCUT, PhD**
Candidate, Faculty of Divinity, University of Cambridge

Honest to God is a provocative pathway of practical equipping. It reveals the way to shed lifeless, non-intimate, inauthentic relationship with God and, instead, to embrace unshackled honesty, transformational freedom, and incredible joy!

—**DR. DWIGHT ROBERTSON**
Founding president of Kingdom Building Ministries and author of *You are God's Plan A . . . and There Is No Plan B*

HONEST TO GOD

BECOMING **BRUTALLY** HONEST
WITH A GRACIOUS GOD

JOSH WEIDMANN

MOODY PUBLISHERS
CHICAGO

All Scripture quotations, unless otherwise indicated, are taken from *The Holy Bible, English Standard Version*. Copyright © 2000, 2001 by Crossway Bibles, a division of Good News Publishers. Used by permission. All rights reserved.

Scripture quotations marked NIV are taken from the *Holy Bible, New International Version*®. NIV®. Copyright © 1973, 1978, 1984 by Biblica, Inc.™ Used by permission of Zondervan. All rights reserved worldwide. www.zondervan.com

All websites listed herein are accurate at the time of publication, but may change in the future or cease to exist. The listing of website references and resources does not imply publisher endorsement of the site's entire contents. Groups, corporations, and organizations are listed for informational purposes, and listing does not imply publisher endorsement of their activities.

Published in association with literary agent Jenni Burke of D. C. Jacobson & Associates, an Author Management Company, www.DCJacobson.com

Editor: Christopher Reese
Interior Design: Smartt Guys design
Cover Design: Maralynn Rochat
Cover Image: Man holding paper in front of face-iStock
Author Photo: David Gaston

Library of Congress Cataloging-in-Publication Data
Weidmann, Josh.
 Honest to God : becoming brutally honest with a gracious God / Josh Weidmann.
   p. cm.
 ISBN 978-0-8024-0359-9
 1. Spirituality. 2. Hypocrisy—Religious aspects—Christianity.
 3. Christian life. I. Title.
 BV4501.3.W4223 2012
 248.4—dc23
                    2011051938

We hope you enjoy this book from Moody Publishers.
Our goal is to provide high-quality, thought-provoking books and products that connect truth to your real needs and challenges. For more information on other books and products written and produced from a biblical perspective, go to www.moodypublishers.com or write to:

Moody Publishers
820 N. LaSalle Boulevard
Chicago, IL 60610

3 5 7 9 10 8 6 4

Printed in the United States of America

FOR MOLLY

You've displayed for me the value of vulnerability.
You have brought me to be more intimate with Christ every day
that I've known you.
Your love has become my home and your passion
for God's truth has kept me there.

Thank you for seeing me as I am and loving me all the same.

I love you.

HONESTY IS NOT AN END IN ITSELF

A few years ago, my life was rocked by a fifteen-word phrase. At the beginning of a three-hour class at Moody Bible Institute, my professor turned my world upside down with this statement:

Honesty is not an end in itself—it is a means to our own transformation.

I clung to every word of explanation he gave, but as soon as he moved on from this statement, I tuned out. I was so distracted by the power of that concept:

Honesty . . .

with myself, others, and especially with God . . .

leads to change.

For the next two hours and fifty-some minutes, I only half listened to what was probably a very good lecture and mulled over that phrase. I wrote it over and over in my notes. I doodled it. I pondered it. And then, I tested it. If it was true that honesty is a means to transformation, then whatever I was honest about should begin a change in my life. So I started being completely honest . . .

- with myself
- with my friends
- with my family
- even with God

And things started to change. The fresh air of truth breathed life into parts of my heart and mind that were otherwise dead. It was invigorating as I began to experience what I'd hardly dared hope was possible! But seeing my individual life affected by honesty was not enough to make me believe my professor's statement was true. I wanted to know if openness was something that could set others free as well.

If you could ask anything . . .
Say anything . . .
Tell anything . . .
If you could get really honest to God . . .
Would you?

These were the words I used when I began a postcard campaign, inviting others to join me and be changed by radical and unflinching honesty. By placing hundreds of self-addressed postcards in everyday places, I asked people to put words to things they had never voiced to another soul. I invited them to speak the doubts they'd never dared to whisper, to unpack the questions and thoughts that had been burning but had never found a way out . . . until now.

The only caveat was absolute honesty.

I left the postcards in gas stations, airports, and restaurants. I even placed them in churches I passed randomly on the road. I stuck them in pew Bibles and hymnals. I left them in coffee shops and bookstores. I mailed them to other college students all around the world. When I spoke at a church or rally, I would hand one to everyone in attendance. The front part of the cards explained the concept; the other side was blank for people to return with their own question or statement. I never intended to respond to them—postcards have no return address—I just wanted to invite others to begin a search for freedom through honesty.

My goal was to find an answer to the question: When people are honest with God, can it really be a catalyst to life alteration?

One by one, the postcards came back. Scrawled across them I found questions, confessions, statements of belief about God, tragedy, faith, life:

- "Even though I know it's wrong, I continue to say mean, hurtful, judgmental things. I hate this weakness in me. Heavenly Father, please lift this burden from me."
- "I need to stop with the porn and start praying to God."
- "I have pushed You away. Wanted to do things my way. I've done sinful things in my life to satisfy the loneliness I feel. Please forgive me, Lord."
- "We had an abortion twenty-six years ago. Our two other babies would've had another brother."
- "I don't want to necessarily say that I'm mad at God, but it feels like He knows our family is falling apart and He's doing nothing about it. He has to know this is not the best. Why doesn't He do something about it? I feel so helpless!"

I began to see that honesty, if the heart behind it is willing, can allow God to come in and replace or remove things that have been tucked away in the closet for far too long. Openness with God can bring renewal relationally, emotionally, and most importantly, spiritually.

I believe that by being vulnerable before God, we can all begin a journey toward truth. When we stop keeping secrets and constructing walls, our lives are opened for makeovers, additions, and replacements from the very One who created us in the first place. Imagine the difference God's divine hand could have in your areas of weakness, doubt, and shame. Think for a moment about the relief that would come if you knew that being honest with God would allow you to stop fighting to be that "better person" you desire to be because God is making you the person *He knows* you can be. He created you, so He knows you better than you know yourself. Though this journey is sometimes painful, it is also transformational, as I have experienced firsthand.

In the following pages you will find the record of my journey through Scripture and life to find the way that honesty—especially with God—results in lasting change. I've studied the honest men and women in the Bible and the bold statements they made to God. By their example, I have been able to learn how to be honest with God the right way—not arrogantly, but humbly opening my life to the repair work of my Creator.

My prayer is that as you observe these authentic confessions and conversations with God, it will lead you to genuine alterations in your life, as it has in mine. Once you have been truly open to the tender hand of our gracious God, you will readily pull off the bandages of life's wounds in an effort to find lasting healing. You will long for depth and never want to go back to a dried-up prayer life of filler statements. You'll dust off the sneaking suspicion that if God knew the real you—what you really think and feel—He wouldn't accept you. Your authenticity before God will lead to greater intimacy with Him, a more secure identity for yourself, and even a greater confidence around others. All of this comes from confessing your trust in the only One who deserves it and being willing to see who God is and who you really are before Him.

Maybe you're really not sure. Maybe you really do think God is out to get you, or at the very least just tolerates your existence. That's okay for now, but I'm asking you, pleading with you, to just consider: What if there's a different way to see yourself, your life, and God? What if your life really could be better, freer, *more* than what you've always thought it was?

As we begin, allow the fragments of your life to be laid bare. It may feel awkward, but we won't be lingering in the shadows for long. Let's find our way to the freedom of true transformation.

PART ONE

REACHING
FOR REAL

CHAPTER 1

RAW KNEES AND A RAW SOUL

HONESTY IS MORE THAN BLURTING AND BLABBING

Think about *raw* for a minute. It's just a basic three-letter word that indicates something not processed or tidy. Raw has a multitude of uses:

Raw fruit

Raw meat

Raw vegetables

Raw knees

A raw deal

Raw concept

Raw feelings

Its different uses communicate different nuances but similar concepts:

Uncooked

Unheated

Unaltered

Without skin
Underdone
Underdeveloped
Rare
Unprocessed
Unrefined
Untreated

When something is raw, it's in its most natural state.

For this very reason I fear the state of raw in my own life. If I'm in my natural state—before people or God—it means the real me is exposed. And if something about that is undesirable or unappealing, there is nothing to blame it on except for me, the real me. If I can't even be comfortable with who I am, then how am I to expect others—or even my Creator—to be okay with the *raw and real* me? You see, when we think we are undesirable, or even less than that, we will project that onto others' perception of us.

Isn't it ironic that we often find it easier to be something we are not, rather than simply being who we are? It's like we have to *try* to be natural. We have to work hard just to be ourselves. We become so worried about what others will think of us that we act the way we think they want us to act, rather than just being who we are. In most cases, we try hard to be acceptable when we are already accepted. If we are going to expose ourselves for the sake of growth, then we must move from a place of perceived security to vulnerable authenticity with ourselves and with God.

A raw piece of meat shrink-wrapped in your grocer's meat department makes no effort to be raw, it simply is. Yet it sits there to be looked at, examined, poked, measured for fat content, and then either chosen or left in the cooling display because the steak next to it was a bit more lean. So is that it? Is that the feeling you and I get when it comes to being totally honest? Do we fear our flaws may be the very reason that man or God will choose to give attention to someone else? Maybe we're just smarter than a piece of angus, and we realize *if* we display our true selves, we might be misunderstood and left unloved? When we are completely honest, we have to admit we're afraid that our weaknesses will be exposed and we may not be accepted the way we really are.

To me, raw feels something like this . . .

FORTUNE COOKIE FAIL

I hadn't even finished my Szechwan Noodles and Chengdu Chicken before I ripped open the cellophane wrapper to get the odd-shaped cookie out of its package. I always open the fortune cookie before I finish, for the fun of reading whatever random message it may carry. I cracked the cookie in the middle and pulled out the small strip of paper.

What would the message hold for me? What "profound" insight would it carry for my life?

I could hardly wait.

The message read, "Your Confidence Will Soon Bring You Great Success."

I flattened the paper in front of me and continued with my chicken and lo mein.

Success. All right! I could use some success. I read the phrase again: confidence would bring success. Hmm. Confidence. Confidence? *What confidence?* I thought. *Are you kidding? I don't have confidence. I only wish I had confidence.*

I began to turn it around in my mind. If I had confidence then perhaps I *could* have great success. So maybe that's my problem? Do I just doubt myself too much? Is that why life seems so hard? Suddenly I was caught in a wave of self-doubt. The cookie was right. I needed confidence before I could ever have success.

The next morning after a restless night of sleep, I realized a profound but startling truth:

THAT COOKIE DOESN'T KNOW ME.

That fortune cookie didn't give a flying spicy cucumber about me. It had no idea who I was. It knew nothing about my life, my personality, my hopes, dreams, fears, or ambitions. In fact, that cookie didn't know anything about anything. It was just a hard, bland lump of sugar and flour.

But how often do I cling to a religion filled with fortune-cookie sayings? Ever heard any of these?

"Christians aren't perfect, just forgiven."

"God has a wonderful plan for your life."

"Jesus is the answer to everything."

"No Jesus, no peace. Know Jesus, know peace."

"When you can't sleep, don't count sheep. Talk to the shepherd."

"Life is fragile; handle it with prayer."

These sayings have no idea who I am. They don't know my situation or the deeper issues in my life. True faith requires something deeper—answers that can't be contained in one bumper-sticker phrase. These phrases may have worked when I was a kid, but the older I get, the more I need something substantial to sustain my faith.

What are the deeper answers? What will be required of me to get them?

I have to let go of clichés I've clung to—you know, the scraps of truth too small to keep me afloat in the midst of life's storms.

So let's start here . . .

Unprocessed.

Unrefined.

Unaltered.

Untreated.

Raw.

> Raw honesty requires me to
>> bare my soul before a holy God.

NAKED, BUT NOT FOR STREAKING

Raw honesty is not meant . . .

> . . . to shock.

> . . . to grab attention.

> . . . to expose what shouldn't be.

> . . . to appear cool or interesting.

None of these should be a goal.

The real point of raw honesty is illustrated for me in a memory from my high school years—one involving my own sense of nakedness. I was only a freshman, but I wasn't too naive to know something was up.

At church youth group, we usually sat in chairs facing the front of the room. That night there were no chairs to be found. The old, scrawny pulpit was even hidden. It was as if all the familiarity had been removed. Tonight was going to be something different. That evening we sat in a circle on the floor. It was kind of uncomfortable, actually. I could see everyone, and everyone could see me. I felt vulnerable, out in the open, and defenseless.

Our youth pastor sat down, filling the gap at the top of the circle. The room silenced, and we all gave him perplexed looks. You could tell he was enjoying watching us squirm in the mystery of not knowing what would happen next.

At first I thought we were in trouble. The only times things seemed to change around youth group were when something serious needed to be said. There was no snoozing or note-passing like usual. Our youth pastor obviously was going to say something out of the ordinary.

"Tonight, you get to share your doubts," he said. "I'm not going to preach. It's your turn to talk. I'm not here to answer your questions or make your doubts go away. I just want to allow you to say whatever you need to say about church, faith, God, Christianity, or life."

There was a long pause.

I remember thinking, *This is so awkward. Did we all sign up for some counseling lab? Are there hidden cameras in the walls?* I didn't think anyone was going to say anything. I thought this was one of our youth pastor's games gone bad—like the time Jared had to go to the ER because he choked on a piece of marshmallow while trying to say "chubby bunny" with fourteen giant marshmallows in his mouth.

Who was going to talk first and save our youth pastor the embarrassment?

Ashlee, of course. She was the pastor's daughter—she had to set an example. I don't remember exactly what she said, but I know it broke the ice. It was probably some superspiritual question like, "I am not sure what to make of the hypostatic union—how could Christ be both man and God at the same time?" Nonetheless, I was grateful that *someone* spoke.

After that, an avalanche of questions came. No answers were given. It was like we all were just comforted to know other people had doubts too. When I voiced a question and heard someone else make that subtle *hmmm* sound or saw someone nod his head in understanding, it felt good to know I wasn't alone.

These were the types of questions we asked:

Why should I pray anyway, if God already knows what I'm going to say?
If God hates divorce, does that mean He hates my mom and dad?
How many times can you sin the same sin before God just washes His hands of you?

Why do I feel miserable so much of the time—can all this Christianity stuff really make me feel better?

Is that really, really nice Mormon girl in class next to me actually going to burn in hell for all eternity?

Looking back on it now, I realized there were two types of honesty taking place that night. Some got it. Some didn't.

Like Thom. He asked, "Am I still a virgin if I touch my girlfriend's breasts?" When he said it, he had the cheesiest grin on his face. Not only was this question uncouth, but we all knew who his girlfriend was, so it was completely uncomfortable. She was right there, practically sitting in his lap.

It was suspicious why Thom asked what he did. To me, it was pretty obvious he mostly just liked saying "breasts" in youth group and getting away with it. Who knows if he really cared if he was still a virgin or not. To me, his statement was more about saying something shocking to get attention. (Sure enough, people talked about it for weeks.)

Though I may not have fully grasped this at the age of fifteen, that was the beginning of my journey to understanding that there are two types of honesty. One type seeks to be nothing more than attention grabbing. The other type bears all for the sake of exposing what needs to be changed.

There's a fine line between true courage and plain old immaturity.

Honesty has to be far more than just being honest.

It must result in change. Often that change is in us.

When we are truly open with God, it must be for the sake of transformation. The transformation comes when we allow God to take our thoughts, feelings, and beliefs and reconstruct them around the right view of who He is and how He is moving in our lives. It means holding our life before the gospel and the nature of God and seeing ourselves in light of it.

Because God already knows everything, by being honest with God we're saying, "Look, I'm going to be totally bare before Truth Himself. He knows everything about me anyway—I'm just acknowledging that. By being vulnerable with God, I'm going to allow my beliefs, opinions, and doubts to be conformed to what really is, not just what I have accepted to be true."

Honesty is never an end in itself;
it is a means to our own transformation.

This statement can be true only if our love for, trust in, and fear of God is the driving force behind our authenticity with God. If those things aren't driving us, then we must dare to be honest even about that and invite the truth of God's Word and the power of His Spirit to help. A lack of the right perspective of who God is will only leave us saying things for the point of being heard, not with the goal of being transformed. Openness with God does not bring change just because we blurted something to Him—that would be self-serving and give us too much credit. Rather, frankness with God allows Him to grab the very thing we are struggling with out of our little white-knuckled hands and replace it with the truth He desires us to cling on to. This replacement leads to change but can only be initiated by our willingness to let go and be honest. And once we are honest, He takes our open palms and gives us Himself—the greatest gift He could give. Love, grace, mercy, justice, patience, kindness—and every other attribute—will now consume our lives in place of the once trite, painful, and entrapping things. There is nothing more amazing and fulfilling than that!

VALUABLE VULNERABILITY

So did true honesty happen that night at my youth group?

I think so. For about an hour, most of us forgot anyone else was in the room. We said things we had kept under wraps far too long. Most of us didn't do it to get attention. In fact, when we came again to the realization we weren't alone, many of us turned a little red. It felt awkward being that raw. I felt vulnerable. But we spoke anyway, because we wanted to start walking down the road to authenticity. Many of us spoke with a quiet desperation in our voices, communicating, "If I really knew the answer to what I'm asking, it would change my life."

That is true honesty.

But honesty *without* the goal of transformation is nothing more than blabbing, gossip, or self-excavation.

Honesty must move you to bare your soul. It means that you have to pull your skeletons of doubt out of the closet and into the fresh air of faith. Then flesh will begin to grow. Life will reside where death once dominated.

Bitterness will change to forgiveness.

Apathy will be transformed to action.

Cynicism will turn to enthusiasm.

Are you willing to face that type of honesty? Are you sure you really want to change? Hang on. Before you answer too quickly . . .

Consider the weight of this statement:

When you are truly honest to God, it is

impossible

to stay the same.

CHAPTER 2

FROM EXPOSED IN MY NAKEDNESS TO
COVERED IN HIS HOLINESS

Let's have a show of hands—who has had a "naked-in-public" dream? Come on, admit it. I bet just about everyone has, including me.

You know the one: You show up for a big presentation at work or school, or you're riding a bicycle through rush hour, or working the first day of a new job, and you suddenly realize everyone is looking at you strangely. Some of them laugh; others turn away in shocked indignation. Puzzled, you look at yourself and discover—*Horror!*—you forgot to put on clothes that morning. All day long you've been cruising around stark naked. *Exposed!*

For me, this kind of dream usually shows up when I am under unusual stress:

Overworked . . .

Overwhelmed . . .

Over my head with some task or project . . .

Or feeling guilty over something I don't want other people—or God—to see.

It's my subconscious mind's way of tapping me on the shoulder to say, "Hey, Buddy, you're not nearly as together as you pretend to be." The dream details will differ, but if you are like me, it always ends the same way: You *run*. You *hide*. You grab anything you can to cover your nakedness. You wake up in a panic, desperate to get away from all those accusing eyes. What a relief to find out it was only a dream!

Or was it?

The truth is, most of us go our whole lives feeling "exposed," even when we are awake. It is an inescapable dimension of human nature. Deep down we know we don't measure up, and we live with the constant, nagging fear that we'll be found out at any moment. We feel naked on the *inside* and there is nothing to be done about it, no matter how fast we run or how cleverly we hide. It doesn't matter who you are: rich or poor, pretty or plain. Sure, there's the occasional day when things go our way and we feel like the king or queen of the world—until the next time we look in the mirror or slow down long enough to be alone with our thoughts. Then we hear that familiar voice accusing, "Who are you kidding? Everyone is laughing at you. Want to know why? Because you're *naked*—all your blemishes are exposed and you have nowhere to hide!"

Doesn't this sound a bit familiar?

Of course, this common human condition isn't a recent development. It is not simply the result of the pent-up stress of modern living. No, the story of humanity *began*, literally days after creation, with the mother of all "naked-in-public" nightmares. Just ask Adam and Eve. Here's their story.

TROUBLE IN PARADISE

In the beginning God created the heavens and the earth, and it wasn't just good—it was *awesome*! Mountains and verdant valleys; rivers, lakes, and oceans; a playful and wondrous variety of plants, animals, and fishes; the sun, the moon, and the stars in the sky. It was a perfect paradise, a lush and fertile garden called Eden. And on the sixth day of His work, God created something really special— *people*, made in His own image, and after His own heart—a man and a woman who would inherit all this newly created splendor and live there in perfect, unhindered communion with the earth, with each other, and most importantly, with God.

And it worked! For who knows how long Adam and Eve frolicked freely in paradise with God Himself. Like a dad and kids rolling in the grass together, spotting shapes in the clouds, telling stories and laughing, they were utterly absorbed in each other's company. In those days Adam and Eve were every bit as holy as the Creator Himself—what could be better than that? Oh, and there is one minor detail I left out: Adam and Eve were naked. As a pair of jaybirds.

But here's the cool part: they were so free, so accepted, so innocent, they didn't *know* they were naked. They didn't even know what naked *was*. Why should they? What was there to hide, and from whom? God created them as they were, perfect and complete in His eyes, so that's how they saw themselves as well. It is like when my wife allows our toddler to run loose in the backyard to play on a summer day—no diaper, no clothes, and absolutely no awareness he is naked. What difference does it make when there are butterflies to chase, sprinklers to run through, and popsicles to eat? What a life!

Of course, it would be nice if the story had ended there: "And humanity lived happily ever after." But we all know the next chapter in the saga. Inevitably, Adam and Eve blew it. Like most toddlers, they had a small issue with boundaries. Well, *boundary*, really, because God placed only one restriction on them. They could eat anything they wanted in the whole garden—anything at all—except for the fruit of the Tree of Knowledge of Good and Evil. He warned them that, if they did this, they'd surely die.

Eventually, along came the Serpent—Satan—who had his own lurid history of rebellion against God. He said, "Really? You buy all of that? Here's what I think—God doesn't want you to eat that fruit because He knows that, when you do, you'll be just like Him. Surely you won't die. Just take a bite." Who knows how many times the Serpent had already come around to pitch this con to Adam and Eve? A hundred? A thousand? Maybe this was the very first. In any case, on that day something in his argument appealed to Eve. She was convinced, and she took the fruit and ate it. Adam was right there and didn't mind helping himself as well.

Bam! *Pow!* Sure enough, their bodies *didn't* die; but something on the inside did. Oh, their bodies carried on the appearance of life for some time, but deep within, something was terribly wrong. In retrospect we know God hadn't been talking about immediate literal death, but the end of innocence, the end of the holy life they had known. Suddenly—and here's the part you'll be able to identify with—they realized they were naked and had been all along. Now, just as the tree's name implied, they knew the difference between right and wrong—and saw that they had been *wrong*. They were exposed and vulnerable for the first time ever. Only moments ago they'd enjoyed perfect safety and freedom in God's garden.

If our present-day dreams are any guide, what do you think they did next? You got it. They *ran.* They *hid.* They grabbed the first leaf handy and covered themselves to escape their shame. And we've been hiding ever since.

You see, eventually, we all blow it too. Why? Well, it actually has nothing to do with our actions or the poor intentions of our heart.

Because of Adam's and Eve's decision to defy God, sin is now a part our very nature. "Therefore, just as sin came into the world through one man, and death through sin, and so death spread to all men because all sinned" (Romans 5:12).

All men. No exceptions.

That fact makes us feel as naked as Adam. We may not even know why we feel so exposed, but it doesn't matter why. We just know we don't measure up for some reason, so we run and hide—from ourselves, from each other, and above all from God. Adam and Eve retreated to the closest hiding place they could find. They sat under the cover of dense undergrowth and dirt of the garden, desperate to remain unseen. They made themselves small and quiet and hoped the all-seeing, all-knowing God who lovingly crafted them out of the dust wouldn't see them cowering there in the dirt.

They hid from Love Himself. "I heard the sound of You in the garden, and I was afraid," Adam said to God. He grossly underestimated the presence of God by thinking he could hide. Even worse, he said he was afraid because he was naked—"That is why I hid myself." I am sure this fear was not only of God's impending judgment, but also the terror of thinking he'd lost the intimate relationship he loved the most. Now he stood bare with nothing to his name except the shame on his face. He hid like a kid crouched behind the couch after eating the forbidden candy bar, with the evidence of chocolate smeared all over his face. I've been there; I've felt Adam's fear. After the deed is done, I can't help but quiver in my soul to think I just disappointed my Creator whom I love to please.

You and I don't live in a garden, but we still have our covers. Oh, our fig leaves may be Chuck Taylors or skinny jeans or may resemble the nearest Starbucks corner armchair. We use the camouflage of modern-day life to avoid being exposed for who we really are. You and I are not so different from Adam and Eve. Let me suggest that the ways you cover your own sense of nakedness and the manner in which you hide are some of the most important things to recognize about yourself on this road to transformation:

1. We don't answer the phone. Typically, the first thing to go when you feel guilty and ashamed over something you've done to someone is communication. Sure, we have our excuses for hitting the ignore button on the phone—it will be a long conversation, I'll call them back when I can focus, or if I just ignore it, they'll forget. But the truth is, as much as you might long for a chance to say you're sorry, the risk of being blasted by the other's anger and hurt is too great. You'd rather lay low for a while. Your relationship with God is no different. In fact, with Him we have even more incentive to take cover when we think we've messed up. Feeling naked in public among other people is bad enough, but in front of the Almighty, before whom even angels fall on their faces? No thanks. Run. Hide. Above all: *avoid being caught alone with God in prayer, Bible reading, church, or all of the above.*

2. Steer clear of people who might see right through us. Picture this: It has been a hard day and you just want to get home to a relaxing evening. First, you must stop off at the grocery store. Just as you turn your cart down the frozen food aisle, who turns in at the other end? The little league baseball coach you promised to help with the team this year and then changed your mind—without telling him that. There are even a few unreturned voice mails on your phone you've been "meaning to get to" for some time. Truth is, you broke your word and bailed, and now you feel terrible about it. He hasn't seen you yet as you're trying to hide behind other shoppers. What do you do? Approach him and confess that you blew it and offer to make it up somehow? Maybe. If you are like most people, though, your first impulse is to pull a quick U-turn and spend the next fifteen minutes in the cat food section until the coast is clear again. And you don't even have a cat.

Here's the "run and hide" rule when God is the one we'd rather not bump into: *avoid worship, church, and maybe even Christians, altogether.*

3. Give them the old "razzle-dazzle." Sometimes, when running and locking yourself in the closet won't work, the best strategy is to hide in plain sight. This involves not only pretending your offenses never happened, but making a show of being the "cool-calm-and-collected-Christian" so that people would never believe *you of all people* could do or think anything wrong. Piety is an excellent smokescreen. Tireless service and "good works" make wonderful camouflage. Bottom line: *perform however you must to avoid admitting your feelings of guilt and shame.*

AN ALTERNATE ENDING

Here's where we left off in the story: Adam and Eve were ashamed of their nakedness; they ran and hid. Then God got angry, kicked them out of paradise, and cursed them (and us) with a life of pain and scraping in the dirt to survive. We've all been suffering miserably ever since, with dying and going to heaven being our only hope of relief. End of story, right? Isn't this more or less what most of us believe? It must be. Why else would we still be running and hiding from God like our lives depend on it?

No, that is not the way the story ends. God knew very well what happened. Yet before He got around to discussing the inevitable consequences of what Adam and Eve had done, He did something we typically overlook when remembering the story: *He went looking for them.* He could have given them the silent treatment, or let them sit in the bushes and rethink their lives for a while, or simply got up and left the garden for good. But He didn't. Even after their willful rebellion, He sought them out.

"Where are you?" He asked.

All Adam could mutter back from the foliage was, "I heard You in the garden, and I was afraid, because I was naked, and I hid myself."

Crazy, right? Adam hid from God. Even more crazy—God knew where he was and didn't leave him in hiding but pursued him all the more.

The mind-blowing truth is this: He's still looking. God sent Jesus, at great cost, to find each and every one of us—to find *you*. Not so that He could haul you back into court and throw the book at you. He sent His Son to invite you to quit running and come home again. The garden of God's unconditional love, forgiveness, and acceptance of you still exists. His plan, by the power of grace made possible by Jesus Christ, is to do away with "nakedness" entirely, and restore us to holiness in His presence. The proof of this was in the prophetic events immediately following the fall of man.

After they had defied God, He went to find them *and* clothe them. "The Lord God made for Adam and for his wife garments of skins and clothed them" (Genesis 3:21). How gracious was God at that moment to not leave them exposed but to kill his own Creation, a few wild beasts, and use their skins to cover Adam's and Eve's exposed backside with a sacrifice. He did the same thing for all of us, not by killing an animal but by allowing His innocent Son to be killed. He sought us and sent His Son as a sacrifice to cover us. All this displays the gracious invitation for us to be honest with Him.

The purpose of being honest with God is to be taken from our embarrassing nakedness and to be clothed in Christ's perfection. That's why honesty is worth the potential discomfort and anxiety—to have the promise of returning to close fellowship and a life sustained by grace.

God's looking.

"Where are you?"

CHAPTER 3

FEAR ITSELF AND FEAR OF GOD

THE RECIPE FOR HONESTY WITH GOD
HAS TWO MAIN INGREDIENTS: FAITH AND FEAR

Picture this: I'm a kid, about ten years old. I'm sitting in a semicircle on the carpeted floor in a Sunday school room with fifteen other kids. The teacher—a brave, dedicated woman who faithfully herds us each week through crafts and games and snacks—has finally settled us down to hear the day's lesson. As usual, we squirm and whisper, and think mostly about how to get a second helping of cookies and juice. Even so, she patiently presents a Bible story and explains what it means for God's people—or, in our case, His rowdy *kids*.

The featured Scripture verse for the day is Proverbs 9:10: "The fear of the Lord is the beginning of wisdom, and the knowledge of the Holy One is insight."

Well, pity the poor teacher because "wisdom" and "knowledge" are pretty vague concepts to a bunch of fourth graders still trying to get a grip on long division and the difference between a subject and a verb. But "fear"? Now *that* we understand. Even at our tender age we've already spent years afraid of the dark, bullies at school, and being punished for lying about who broke the window in the garage. The list of our fears is long.

So it is naturally a setback to our fledgling understanding of who God is and how much He loves us to be told that we should "fear" Him. We must have slightly horrified looks on our faces, because the teacher immediately attempts to comfort us and clear up our confusion.

"You never need to be *afraid* of God, but you must learn to *fear* Him," she says cryptically.

Huh?

The girl next to me chimes in, "I'm afraid God will make lightning strike our house when my brother yells God's name with cusswords at my parents."

From there it is all downhill. The class ends with our understanding of the fear of the Lord still out of reach—though from that day on I suspect we all began to think of God more as the school principal than the benevolent Grandfather we thought we knew.

A LITTLE PERSPECTIVE

Years later, I must admit the difference between being *afraid* of God and properly *fearing* Him can still seem pretty fuzzy at times—like a riddle that appears to have no logical solution. How can the dreaded, wasting emotion we know as *fear* ever lead to "wisdom" and "insight"? What room is there for love and trust in a relationship defined by fear? Most important of all: How can I ever feel safe enough to be completely *honest* with God if I'm also *afraid* of Him?

How, indeed?

Here's an important point: *one of the biggest reasons we avoid honesty with God is that we are afraid of His reaction to what we have to say.*

Our human relationships have reinforced this fear time and again. Chances are, at some point, someone has said to you, "It's okay, just tell the truth. I promise I won't get angry." How does that usually turn out, especially when you confess something you've done to offend that person? Most of the time he goes ahead and gets angry or feels hurt anyway, right? Being human, he can't help it—and we come to expect the same thing from God, no matter what assurances we've heard to the contrary.

But as I will remind you many times in these pages, *God isn't like us!* With Him, we never have to be afraid of the sucker punch. He'll never invite us to come to Him with one hand while concealing a baseball bat in the other.

Paradoxically, living with a healthy "fear of the Lord"—the attitude the writer of the proverb had in mind—will always make it easier to tell Him what we truly think and feel. That's because it puts our lives into proper perspective in relation to Him. It welcomes and embraces the fact that He isn't like us—an incredibly comforting thought when you consider how often people have let you down. To bring this idea into sharper focus, let's try describing it with some different words.

The fear of the Lord is:

- An attitude of awe, respect, reverence, and praise in response to seeing God rightly
- The desire to please Him above all others
- Unflinching allegiance to Him, even in the face of adversity
- The willingness to abandon our will to His in all circumstances
- The ability to treat the unseen kingdom of God as more important than the material kingdoms of the world

When you put it like *that*, it doesn't sound much like "fear" at all, does it? More like a deeply committed relationship with someone you love very much. In this light it's easy to see how living by these principles could lead to greater wisdom, insight, and blessing—and even *honesty* with God.

Problem solved, right? Just do all that stuff, and the fear of the Lord is a snap. Actually, I doubt anyone is thinking *that* right now. If you are like me, you are thinking: *I could never do that! I'll forget and revert to old habits. It's impossible!* While this extended definition of the fear of the Lord looks simple enough on paper, that doesn't mean it's *easy* to put into practice in the trenches of life, where there are many other things to fear in addition to God. But is it impossible? No.

To prove it, let me tell you a gripping tale of adultery, power, treachery, murder, and judgment. We've heard stories like this before. A simple click through the nightly news will reveal to us good people (or those we perceived as good) falling into scandal. We've even heard the stories of Christian ministers consumed by actions contradictory to the titles they carry. At the beginning of my pastoral ministry, I heard for eighteen consecutive months about prominent pastors (heroes of mine) falling into crazy sin. We've grown numb to stories of corruption, but allow your innocence to return and let this story surprise you for two reasons: First, because it is in the Bible. Second, the main character is someone you'd never believe was capable of such crimes as these. He's been called "a man after God's own heart." How could he be a shameless voyeur, a lustful adulterer, a backstabbing schemer, a cowardly murderer, and still have God's affection? How could King David himself make such a mess of things? Let's find out.

A SERIES OF BAD CHOICES

Winter was finally over in Israel, and David had a bad case of spring fever. It was the season when kings usually packed up and went off to battle. Indeed, David had already sent his forces into the field to resume the ongoing war against the Ammonites but for some reason that year he stayed behind in Jerusalem. Maybe he was tired of constant warfare and needed a break. Maybe he was bored. Maybe he was restless.

In any case, while his soldiers slept on the ground, ate bad food, and risked their lives for his sake, David spent his springtime lounging around the palace. One day, while taking a midday walk on the roof, he happened to see, atop an adjacent building, a woman taking a bath. Not just any woman. She was *beautiful*. Suddenly his wandering and idle mind fixed itself on a new goal: get that lady!

Acting on this impulse, David made some discreet inquiries and got back bad news: her name was Bathsheba and she was married to Uriah, one of his most loyal captains. No doubt David had already imagined receiving Bathsheba as a new wife or concubine, so this must have come as a shock. What to do? Well, if he couldn't marry her, he would at least sleep with her—just once, you understand—to satisfy his longing. After all, he was king, wasn't he? Who could stop him? He'd earned the right to do as he pleased.

So he brought Bathsheba to the palace, slept with her, and sent her back home.

I don't know about you, but so far I'm not seeing any of those "fear of the Lord" qualities we discussed a moment ago. And not much *honesty* either. Mostly this is about David living by the old saying, "If it feels good, do it!" Well, hang in there, because it gets worse before it gets better.

A few weeks later, David gets a sobering message from Bathsheba: "I'm pregnant."

Uh-oh.

Now would be a great time to come clean with God and face the music. But that's not what David does. He is too afraid of the earthly consequences. Having dug the hole this deep, the last thing he wants to do is approach God and start doing the painful work of filling it back in. Mostly, he is afraid of what will happen when Uriah—and everyone else in his kingdom for that matter—learns of his betrayal. No, even now, he is looking for an easier way out of this tight spot.

Sure enough, David arrives at a plan: What if he calls Uriah home from the wars for a few days? After so long in the field, any man would jump at the chance to spend a night in his own bed and sleep with his wife. Then, a few months down the road, nobody will notice that the baby's birthday arrives a little earlier than it should.

Brilliant! He'll get out of this yet.

Except that Uriah, being an exceptionally honorable man, refused to make himself comfortable while his comrades were suffering the hardships of battle without him. You can imagine David's frustration. Not only did Uriah not play into his plan, the man's integrity was a silent rebuke of the king's own choice to kick back at the palace during a time of war. He decided to give it one more try, so he got the man drunk and attempted to trick him into sleeping in his own bed.

It didn't work. Uriah slept in the servants' quarters that night too.

So be it, David must have thought. *You brought this on yourself.* He sent word to Joab, commander of the army, to place Uriah in the thick of the battle and then strand him there to be killed.

Wow. David had forgotten the first rule of getting yourself out of a hole: *stop digging*! Picture a kid who has spilled grape juice on the family room carpet. Rather than ask for help—and face Mom's wrath—he decides to clean it up himself with a kitchen towel and a little water. But the more he scrubs, the bigger the stain grows until it's finally the size of a beanbag chair. That's how it usually goes with us. We get into trouble because we think we can manage life on our own and then make matters worse by trying to "fix it" when things go wrong.

Joab complied with David's order and Uriah died. One of Israel's most loyal and respectable captains was a casualty to his king's greed and shame. David had the gall to kill a perfectly good man, beloved husband, and great warrior just to get the woman he wanted. When Bathsheba's period of mourning was complete, David married her. Whew! Disaster was averted—almost. There was just one not-so-tiny problem:

"The thing David had done displeased the Lord" (2 Samuel 11:27).

Nathan the prophet showed up to deliver this message to David. He told the king a sad story about a wealthy man who had everything, but took a poor neighbor's only ewe lamb and slaughtered it to feed his guests. David was outraged, proclaiming that the man deserved to die and that he must repay what he took fourfold because of his lack of pity.

"You are that man," Nathan said and proceeded to tell David everything he had done from the moment he laid eyes on Bathsheba. And David listened. I'm sure he was experiencing a brutal "naked-in- public" moment but he stood still and *listened*.

This entire story—a tragic and twisted trail of mistakes and bad ideas—comes down to this single scene. Will it be a moment of truth? Or a moment when David doubles down on his wager that he can handle things himself? Keep in mind that David had already pronounced judgment in the case: "That man deserves to die!" The stakes are as high as they can be. The impulse David feels to go on running and hiding and trying to wiggle free must be enormous. There are still a few cards left to play. He could have yelled, "Off with his head!" like so many petty tyrants would have done. But he didn't.

What did he say? *"I have sinned against the Lord"* (2 Samuel 12:13).

He was honest, at last.

But what does this mean, really, in this moment? It means he saw himself for the mess he really was in light of God. He faced up to his shame, worry, and manipulation, and owned his guilt before God.

I believe that right then he recognized God's holiness and goodness, His purity and perfection, and His loyalty to David. He saw the Holy Lord, and the reality of what a mess he was before God was apparent. His fear was wrought from a proper perspective of God, not merely a terror of judgment. He acted like a fool, and a fool is foolish because of an inaccurate view of reality. Wisdom is having the right view of reality. Wisdom begins with the fear of the Lord, because that sets the foundation by which we see everything else.

After Nathan's confrontation, David remembered his lifelong allegiance and loyalty to God, and the debt of respect and honor he owed. He recalled his desire to please the Lord and live according to His commandments. He considered God's view to be far more important than the anger and criticism he faced from his fellow humans. In other words, he remembered what it meant to *fear* the Lord more than to be *afraid* of Him. For the first time since the lurid tale began, he feared God more than the possible consequences of his actions.

And it made all the difference in how the story ends. After David's confession, and before Nathan pronounced what those consequences would be, the prophet had this to say: "The Lord also has put away your sin; you shall not die" (2 Samuel 12:13).

Here's the bottom line: *Being honest with God leads to transformation, because it allays our fears and opens our hearts to receive the forgiveness He offers in Christ Jesus.*

David was known as "a man after God's own heart," not because he never made mistakes, and not because God likes to play favorites. David won God's heart because, when everything was on the line, and when he stood utterly naked and exposed in his sin before the Creator, he chose *honesty* over continuing to run and hide. He didn't

only do this once, but made honesty with God his lifestyle, which was a means to transforming change. He allowed his perspective to be readjusted to God's reality time and again, and by doing so remained a man who reflected God's own heart.

CHAPTER 4

MAD AT GOD

LEARNING TO SAY WHAT I THOUGHT COULD NEVER BE SAID

Let me introduce you to my friend Keith. He is probably one of the most welcoming people on the planet, with a smile that will pull you in and a hug that will keep you there. He is a man's man in the way he leads his family, conducts his life, and hangs with the fellas. And if he wasn't already busy with a day job, he could easily be a stand-up comic. His laugh is contagious and his quick wit allows him to conjure random punch lines without skipping a beat.

In addition to all that, I must point out Keith's heart—which is more dedicated to God than just about anyone I know. I imagine he rarely misses daily time with the Lord, and the Scriptures are always on the tip of his tongue. He is one of the most compelling and unhindered reflections of Christ you'll ever meet.

In his early twenties, the love of Keith's life was taken from him because of cancer. As if it weren't enough to have a spouse who was dying, Keith was diagnosed with cancer at the same time. In the midst of saying good-bye to his beloved, he was fighting to stay alive himself. Miraculously, he beat the disease. Against the odds, he fought off the very thing that was trying to kill him.

For more than a decade, Keith was healthy and cancer free. He remarried an amazing woman, Lori, and ended up having two boys: Kip and Bodie. Life was good. But one day Keith noticed he was struggling to swallow. He visited the doctor, who uttered those dreaded words again: "I'm sorry, Keith, you have cancer."

Keith endured very serious forms of cancer—twice. By God's grace, he survived the first bout, astonishing the medical professionals who cared for him. The second time came like the proverbial thief in the night, shocking all of us who knew and loved him. He underwent intense radiation, which had all kinds of awful side effects. The chemotherapy he went through nearly took the life right out of him before the cancer even had a chance.

It has been my privilege to stand beside this courageous man through his excruciating ordeal, but at times I've struggled with questions you ask only when you find yourself or someone you love on death's doorstep. Recently Keith became severely sick, due more to treatments than the cancer itself. I spent the night with him at the hospital so his wife could go home and sleep with their two- and four-year-old boys. In the darkness of the hospital room, with nothing more than the light of blinking machines, I questioned God. I was mad, but I was too scared to admit it. Anger at God is often more subtle than our anger toward other people.

How could God allow such a great man to suffer this way? As I watched Keith sleep, at times gasping for air, everything inside me was screaming, *Oh, God, help! Why are You allowing this?* I would drive away from the hospital in the morning weeping after seeing Lori, Kip, and Bodie returning. I would fiercely mutter in my car as I drove down a crowded boulevard, "Are You kidding me, God?

Why? You can't let this happen!"

When we feel we've been wronged, or someone we love has been hurt, we want a few straightforward answers. We not only want them, but we feel we deserve them. It might be the premature end of a loved one's life or the shattering of a relationship we thought would last forever. Often, our response is to shake a fist toward the One who is supposed to be in control and say,

I thought You loved me? I can't find Your love here.

I don't care if You will be glorified through this; I am in so much pain!

They said at the funeral that You have a plan. How can this be Your plan? Just give me back my mom!

We may feel these things and even think them, but it's rare that we actually communicate such incendiary sentiments to God. We either pretend we're okay while shutting down toward God inwardly, or we blow up and reject God outwardly. If it were another person, no problem—we'd say these things boldly because that person hurt us, so they're going to hear about it. However, when it comes to God, we wordlessly accuse Him, though rarely to His face, until one day we realize we've walked away from Him long ago.

In our darkest moments our heart cries out accusations. The rug has been pulled out from under us, and we are filled with anger. Vengeance. Control. Justification. Explanation. Our soul demands these and more. Yet, instead of straightforward openness, we arm ourselves with the safest and most effective weapon: silence. In our deep hurt, we think, *No, God. No more from You. If this is the way You allow Your children to be treated, no thanks.*

A friend of mine who recently suffered enormous loss said, "I am not sure I can even believe in God anymore. I'm so mad at Him for taking my mom, my dad, and brother and leaving me alone. I don't even want to believe in Him because obviously He is not in control. If anything, it just feels like He is dead to me too."

When we feel God is the one to blame, we don't know what to do with our anger. Stuff it? Pretend it isn't there? Sweat it out at the gym? Make nice with God and hope it'll go away? Most often we only get more upset because we can't believe that God (whom we want to think of as good in the ways we expect) does something or allows something that seems so bad. We feel stuck in our emotions and at a standstill in our honesty. *Can we really be angry with Him? Isn't that just asking for the rest of His wrath to be dumped out on our heads?*

IS IT OKAY TO BE MAD AT GOD?

This week I got a call from a man who discovered his wife had been cheating on him. He told me the whole story about fake business trips that were actually rendezvous with secret lovers. If she hadn't fallen asleep while texting, he would've thought nothing of it. But when the phone kept going off far after she was sound asleep, he decided to take a peek at the text to see who was trying to get ahold of her so persistently. The first text he read drew him, prompting him to scan them all. The little screen held catastrophic words. Suddenly all of her out-of-the-ordinary actions became pieces of concrete evidence. The things she wrote revealed his greatest fear. His anger rose to levels he'd never experienced before. Feeling at a total loss for what to do, he closed the phone and set it back in an inconspicuous place, only to internalize what he had seen.

After he told me all the appalling details, he stopped crying for a minute and started raising his voice over the phone, "She led me to Christ, Josh! Now she cheated on me! She and God are obviously in this together, and I'm beside myself. I know it's not right for me to be angry at her or God. . . ." He trailed off, and I could tell he was trying to figure out what my pastoral response would be. Then he continued, "I'm sure God is not angry with her. I suppose you are going to tell me to forgive and forget, get over it, and keep on loving her—but I can't."

There was a lot I wanted to say in response, but I latched on to one comment in particular. "How are you so sure God is not angry at her?" I asked. "Did He tell you that?"

"Well, no, but He is love, so He can't be angry *and* loving . . . right?"

"Do you still love her, Mike?" I inquired.

"Actually, yes," he replied with a shaky voice.

"Are you angry with her?" I asked.

"I already told you I was," he said.

"So you are saying you love her *and* you are angry with her?"

He thought for a moment. "I guess."

"If you can feel both things," I said, "don't you think God is capable of the same?"

He paused even longer this time and then quietly said, "I suppose so. What's your point?"

"Mike, anger is not an absolute state; it is a feeling about your current reality. For you, the current reality is your wife cheated on you. For God, the current reality is that one of His children sinned against Him. The latter is the bigger deal. Yet God is not One who will stuff His anger and harbor bitterness. So why should you? His anger is righteous—He knows the way things should be and is upset they are not that way. In all His righteous anger, He has proven He will do what it takes to fix it, even if that means allowing His own Son to be killed."

"I guess I just thought God stuffed His anger, especially this side of the cross," he admitted. "I assumed I couldn't be angry or tell God how I really felt because His grace would laugh it off."

As I helped him understand his assumptions were mistaken and explained to him the perfect anger of God, I mentioned passages about Christ's anger toward the hard-hearted (Matthew 11:21–24),

God's wrath toward those who don't believe (John 3:36), and the disobedient (Ephesians 5:6). By the end of our phone call, I challenged Mike to "imitate God," as Ephesians says, and act out his anger correctly (Ephesians 4:26; 5:1). Stuffing his anger was only going to create an ulcer in his soul. I encouraged him to be honest with God about everything before he confronted his wife.

TWO OPTIONS: EXPRESS OR REPRESS

I understand that expressing our anger to or toward God is a lot easier said than done. Most of us accumulate anger and resentment like dirty laundry. At some point those feelings well up and spill over into other areas of our life, creating a deep sense of bitterness for reasons we can't even remember. Anger is universal, but the ways we deal with it vary, and often it is our strategy for handling anger that is wrong rather than the anger itself.

As children, we expressed anger freely. First, it was physically through crying and temper tantrums, and then, with parental guidance, through appropriate verbal expression. As adults we learn how *not* to express anger and instead spend millions on drugs to anesthetize the inevitable pain of keeping it stuffed too long. If anger is suppressed it leaves us in a state of frustration and usually hinders us from seeking divine help.

When it comes to being angry with God, we really have only two choices:

1. **We can talk it out.** We can express to Him how we feel (even if most of this conversation is filled with our screaming).
2. **We can sulk.** In most instances, when we are angry with someone—even God—we avoid them altogether. Sometimes it's easier to pout and have a pity party than actually deal with the issue.

If we don't deal with our anger head-on, it will rear its ugly head in some other way. This can be dangerous. More explosive. Only dig us into a deeper hole. Why do some people kill innocents when they are actually mad at someone else? They didn't go to the source of their anger before it overcame them. The same thing happens spiritually. Not being honest about our anger, frustration, disappointment, or confusion with God will leave others in our lives as casualties in our wake. Believe me, I've been one. I've had people hate me for all sorts of reasons unrelated to me simply because I am a pastor. They've never cleared things up with the God I serve, so they just harbor hatred toward me for reasons they can't even remember.

ANGER KEEPS US FROM TAKING GOD AT HIS WORD

Anger is the aircraft carrier in the fleet of our emotions. Not only because of its massive size, but also its ability to do harm because from it proceeds a multitude of other feelings—grief, sadness, hatred, loss, horror, and doubt. Anger in itself is not necessarily wrong. It is an emotion God has given us, but as with anything He has given us, we must not elevate it higher than Christ. If we allow our lives and hearts to be defined by our anger, we are worshiping at the altar of our emotions, not at the throne of God.

Mary and Martha were faced with the choice of harboring their deep-seated frustration with Christ or clinging to Him for hope. Their brother, Lazarus, was deathly ill, so they sent for Jesus, whom they believed cared about Lazarus too. Yet to their surprise and dismay, He made no effort to get to them quickly. In fact, He stayed away another four days and moved on to a different city rather than running home to be with, and possibly help, Lazarus (see John 11). Imagine how frustrating this must have been for Mary and Martha. They wanted Jesus to respond according to their terms. They were faced with the choice to hold a grudge against Jesus, or to trust Him.

Upon His arrival—*finally*—to Bethany, Martha ran to Him and started playing the "If only. . ." game. Later on, Mary joined in as well. You know the game I'm talking about. It's the game we play when we don't get our way in life, especially from God. We run down a list of "if onlys" with God, telling Him all the ways things would be different *if only* He would have done what we expected. By the time Jesus arrived, Lazarus was dead and buried, and Mary and Martha were sure things would have been different *if only* Jesus had come sooner. You have to admire the honesty of these ladies; in the face of loss they had the guts to cry out before Jesus and share their deep frustration with Him about how they wished He would have acted.

Before Jesus even turned His attention to Lazarus, He took the opportunity to use Martha's honesty as a tool to transform her perspective and deepen her faith. She clearly had great faith in Jesus and acknowledged His unique relationship with God (John 11:21–22). To help her go even deeper, Jesus asked a pivotal question.

"I am the resurrection and the life. . . . Do you believe this?"

"Yes, Lord, I believe," Martha responded.

In their exchange, honesty became the very tool Christ used to lead Martha to a deeper relationship with Him (along with Mary, who also witnessed Lazarus's resurrection). Jesus knew Martha was angry (or at the very least, disappointed), but He also knew that she believed. When honesty before God comes from an attitude of faith and surrender to Him, it creates the opportunity for Him to transform us completely.

Jesus told those nearby to open the tomb, and though Martha hesitated in disbelief, she agreed (vv. 40–41). She had a choice: stay angry at Jesus, fostering resentment and doubt by continuing to play the *if only* game, or take Him at His word, trust Him, and allow Him to change current reality. At this crossroads, Christ asked one simple question:

"Did I not tell you that if you believed you would see the glory of God?"

With that one question, He gave both instruction and promise. The instruction was to believe. The promise was that they would see the glory of God, which would most definitely eclipse any grief, sorrow, pain, doubt, or anger. This is a soothing promise because His glory is the summation of all His character applied to our current situation. Because they chose to believe, the promise came true right then and there, and they saw the glory of God as a dead man got up and walked.

Can you imagine the celebration that took place tomb-side that day? The hugs, laughter, and tears of joy must have been overwhelming for all standing by. I imagine that they were all astonished as they recounted the way Christ had not only raised Lazarus but taken their faith to new heights. In the beginning, they expressed their anger and sorrow to Christ, and in love and gentleness He responded, calling them to greater faith. Their honesty was a tool in the hand of a holy God to transform their "if only" statements into abundant "I believe" declarations.

But not all our stories will end like that. Your mom may never come back from the dead. Cancer may not go away. Your spouse may have no remorse for cheating on you. Yet in all of this God is still God and invites us to trust Him. He will give us glimpses of all He is and can be for us, while inviting us to choose hope and belief in Him.

This whole complex and confusing topic boils down to a few key points:

- Anger is a natural human response, and the emotion of anger isn't bad or wrong in the proper context. If you feel anger, including anger at God, then congratulations, you're human.

- See above and add this important addendum: how you *express* anger can be bad and wrong. There are healthy and unhealthy, constructive and destructive ways to deal with it.
- Giving God the silent treatment and cold shoulder only blocks communication. It may feel good for a while, but it's going to keep you stuck in bitterness. God invites you—wants you—to express your deepest feelings to Him, including your most scorching anger. Don't worry, He won't eject you from His presence if you vent with Him.
- While venting is acceptable, even advisable, blaspheming is not. Expressing our emotions—strongly and intensely, if need be—does not mean it's okay to disrespect and dishonor God.
- Healing happens—spiritually, emotionally, physically—when we address anger rather than avoid it. God, the ultimate healer, wants to walk with you through this process.

We must recall the facts about who God is and His willingness to tend to our deepest pain. In faith we must tell the truth about our anger to the One who has the ability to do something about it. As difficult as it may seem, we must forgive all involved parties, including God. This allows God to work through our pain to help us find hope and healing. If we dare to be this honest with God about how we really feel, we can expect to be changed and experience God's supernatural power.

THE GREASY, GRIMY FEELING COMPELLING US TO HIDE

When my mom, Janet, was sixteen, she planned a surprise twenty-fifth wedding anniversary party for her parents. After a week celebrating in Hawaii, her mom and dad would return to their Denver home for a big bash in their honor.

Mom took on the whopping task almost single-handedly. A crowd of forty partygoers would suddenly descend. The pressure mounted to get everything done.

After a busy week, she faced a full Saturday of frantic cleaning and prepping. She made tons of food, hung streamers, and drew posters. With the hours ticking away, Mom attacked the house—armed with mop, broom, and vacuum—in a cleaning frenzy.

The last chore to tackle was washing the pots, pans, and plates piled high on the kitchen counter. With fifteen minutes until the guests would start arriving, my mom looked at the huge heap of dishes and realized she'd run out of time.

Ever so resourcefully, she grabbed a stack of dishes, hurried to the bathroom down the hall, and stashed them in the shower. A few more back-and-forth trips and the kitchen counter was empty of all that greasy, grimy cookware. Finally, she pulled the crisp, clean shower curtain closed to conceal the makeshift garbage dump.

Soon the mob of friends and family were mingling and milling about, and sounds of conversation and laughter filled the house. Before long, a man named Bernard Kinney asked my mom if he could use the restroom. She somewhat nervously pointed the way to the only one in the house, knowing all the while what hid in the tub. And, apparently, Bernard was a curious type; he couldn't resist a peek into the shower.

Well, well, what have we here? he must have thought.

I envision Bernard emerging from the bathroom with a gleam in his eye and a smug smile on his lips. At six foot four with a floppy toupee atop his bald head, he commanded attention without requesting it. But when he rejoined the other guests, he cleared his throat loudly and announced, "Excuse me, everyone. I have something I'd like to say." Conversation ceased as all the people turned around.

"I've just returned from the bathroom, where I made a most intriguing discovery," he proclaimed, pausing for dramatic effect. "It seems our dear hostess, Janet, has a rather peculiar housekeeping practice. She stowed all the dirty dishes in the shower. Can you believe that? Ha! Well, why wash a dish at a time when you can give them all a bubble bath later!"

Slowly, lightbulbs went on in people's heads as they put two and two together. Nervous chuckles descended into gales of laughter. A few sympathetic souls murmured as the proverbial spotlight shined on my mom's red-hot face.

Surely Bernard was trying to be funny. My mother was a good

sport, laughing along with everyone else—but she was mortified. She had been caught, her ploy revealed. The rest of the evening, and for weeks beyond, she endured jokes and jabs about good house-keeping and the need to repeat home economics class.

I laugh every time I hear that story, mostly because of the way my mom explains good old Bernard Kinney with his toupee, and how she'd give him a piece of her mind if he were still alive. But recently when I was scrubbing my own pile of dishes in a hurry, wishing I could just stash them somewhere, it hit me: the caked-on casserole dishes could represent my faults, and shame comes when these faults are hidden or ignored, and then exposed later.

My mom was certainly embarrassed by her dirty-dish exposure, and this brought a feeling of shame—mostly derived from disap-pointing her parents in a time she wanted to please them the most. In the same way, we often carry shame in our lives. I'm not referring merely to public humiliation; I mean the widespread ploys of con-cealing what we don't want seen. We try to hide our personal garbage, our smelly rubbish, shielding it behind a bleached-white curtain we desperately hope no one will peek behind. We stuff our greasy, grimy dishes in the shower, believing they'll never be noticed.

You know what I'm talking about, don't you? Unless you are a superhero—or at least superhuman—you're probably ashamed of *something*. There's a past failure or present fault that is excruciatingly painful for you to acknowledge and admit. There's something you wouldn't want anyone to know about, something you keep buried deep down within yourself.

Over the years I've spoken with hundreds of people who have opened up and told me their secret failings, chronic struggles, and agonizing wounds. In moments away from eavesdropping ears or in email exchanges away from prying eyes, people have expressed their sense of being chained and constrained, and their desperation to break free. There's a good chance you experience shame if you've ever thought:

I don't measure up to other people's expectations, not to mention God's expectations.

I can't even meet my own standards, so how can I meet God's? I don't like the real me, so why should anyone else?

If people knew the real me, they wouldn't like what they saw.

I act like I've got it all together, but beneath the polished surface I'm a phony and a fraud.

I'm laughing on the outside but dying on the inside.

I imagine God up there on His throne looking down on me with a disappointed look on His face.

If these sound familiar, you are not alone. Shaming ourselves, we become convinced we're no good. Speaking inadequacy over ourselves, we see unworthiness staring back in the mirror. Shame can be a toxic stew of emotions, a feeling of heaviness that weighs on our spirit, dampens our energy, and just plain squashes the zest for life right out of us. Shame eats away at our insides, distorting even how we perceive others are viewing us. It taints our self-respect, tarnishes our confidence.

"Shame is a feeling deep within our being that makes us want to hide," wrote psychologist Jane Middelton-Moz. "We feel suddenly overwhelmed and self-conscious. The feeling of shame is of being exposed, visible, and examined by a critical other. It is the sense that the 'examination' has found the self to be imperfect and unworthy in every way. We hang our heads, stoop our shoulders, and curve inward as if trying to make ourselves invisible." * This is a tough subject for that very reason—we are ashamed of our shame. Are you grimacing? Even writing about it makes me cringe. Because it feels painful, we'd prefer to avoid it. But the reality is, you and I both are

* Jane Middelton-Moz, *Shame and Guilt* (Deerfield Beach, FL: Health Communications, 1990), 14.

controlled to some degree by a sense of shame. Spiritual and emotional wholeness can only happen when we take our dirty dishes out of the shower and get them cleaned properly and thoroughly.

PULLING BACK THE CURTAIN

The challenge of writing a book called *Honest to God* is that the one writing (me) feels duty bound to be honest . . . with you, with myself, and most of all with God. So I'm going to be. I'll tell you a source of my own shame that has caused friction in relationships, self-doubt in myself and, at times, awkwardness in my relationship with God. In 2000, I received the good news that I'd been accepted to Moody Bible Institute to pursue a Bible degree. For all students, acceptance came with a full scholarship, along with the expectation that those enrolled work hard and graduate in four years. The respected and rigorous program called for dedicated and focused students.

I began in January 2001 and made it through three years, with the normal struggles of grappling with theological concepts, learning ancient languages, and writing endless papers. All the while I was traveling on the weekends to speak at events around the country. Yet it seemed manageable and I had three down and one to go . . . or so I thought.

It was time to register for my fourth year, but my speaking schedule was increasing and I was given the opportunity to publish my first book. How could I pass up those golden opportunities? So I decided to leave Moody for one year and pursue a few things I wanted to do. I saw school as a hindrance. I hit the road speaking, moved my stuff out of the dorm and back into my parents' house, and chased my wildest dreams. In addition to my speaking and writing, I attempted another life goal by starting two coffee businesses: one in the Denver Tech Center (which later tanked), the other, ironically, on the campus of Moody Bible Institute, Joe's Coffee Shop (which has thrived). Things were happening for me! All systems were go.

Except for one nagging detail: I hadn't earned my degree, which meant I had not fulfilled my obligation to the school.

After a year's hiatus, I resumed my studies, struggling through classes even as I stayed busy—way too busy—with extracurricular pursuits. All good things, just too many of them. Then when my future mother-in-law got diagnosed with liver cancer and passed away, I was broadsided. So I left school to be with my girlfriend (who is now my wife) and her family for a few weeks while trying to balance the rest of my crazy life and school all at the same time.

Later that year I watched as several friends I'd started with finished the program, earning high grades and faculty praise. I sat through the graduations of my friends, all the while kicking myself for not crossing the stage with them. A few of my professors raised pointed questions, to me and to the administration, about my times away and fragmented schedule. They questioned the wisdom and propriety of taking on so many visible, public ministry endeavors when I hadn't finished my training. In fact, some of my professors pressed so hard that my case was taken before the Academic Standards Committee to review my transcript and attendance in detail.

Clearly, I was floundering. And my GPA plummeted even as my sense of shame skyrocketed.

The next several years saw a pattern emerge: I enrolled in classes, some of which I stuck with and passed, but others I quickly fell behind in and dropped. Several times, when I knew I was going to fail a class, I simply withdrew instead. Better Ws on my record than Fs. I found myself in countless awkward situations, groveling to professors for more time and making excuses for my negligence. One time I hadn't prepared for a big test in Hebrew class, so on every blank space where the answers should have gone, I wrote "I'm so sorry."

All the while, I often felt like I was crawling up to God's throne to pray: "I'm sorry for getting myself in this mess. I'm letting so many people down, and letting You down. How can I fulfill the calling You have for me when I can't even fulfill course requirements?"

Finally I became so sick of saying "I'm sorry" and carrying the shame that I left Moody at the first job offer I received and promised to finish later. Since then I've served in pastoral ministry at three different churches. With each interview process I've had to pull back the curtain of my shame to my unfulfilled promises.

Understand that in my field of professional ministry, academic degrees and credible training are important—extremely important to many people. This ratcheted up my sense of frustration over academic struggles. I lost count of the times at speaking engagements when someone wanted to introduce me as a *graduate* of Moody Bible Institute and I'd have to set the record straight—embarrassing.

Long, painful story made short: At the time of this writing, it is almost ten years since I first enrolled at Moody, and I expect to graduate this year. What was supposed to take me four years took ten. Big relief, for sure, but an even bigger lesson in carrying a burden of shame. Sleepless nights, feeling like a failure, kicking myself for the thousandth time—yeah, I've been there. Along the way I've learned some hard but helpful lessons, and I am a poster child for that line, "If I could do it all over again. . . ."

So I know taking ten years to finish college may be nothing compared to some of the other shame people carry, and believe me, that's not my only area of shame. Some of us can carry guilt for a lifetime over failed marriages, eating disorders, sexual experiences outside of marriage, porn addictions, lies to cover stealing, stealing to cover lies, and the list goes on. But the question is, what are we going to do with all this? Grovel in the guilt of what I woulda-coulda-shoulda done, or allow all this to propel us to a different place with God?

SOME SHAME IS DESERVED AND HELPFUL

The painful truth is that we sometimes feel shame because we've done something shameful. I know that stings a bit, but it's reality. These days no one likes to use the judgmental and oh-so-intolerant word *sin*. But there's no sense skirting around it. We are human beings prone to sin. When we violate God's standard for how He desires us to live and act, we'll justifiably experience shame. When we lie, cheat, gossip, or steal, we're right to feel wrong, and it's good to feel bad. That's because guilt has a way of bringing us to the first step toward repentance. Actions are not the main thing God is concerned about—He is more concerned about our heart. If a heart is to be transformed, and therefore influence our actions, we must allow conviction to prick our conscience and drive us to change. In situations where we feel the weight of our sins, shame is not an enemy but an ally, as strange as that may sound.

God created shame to serve as an internal indicator that our lives are veering off track. This is a warning alarm that announces trouble or danger, a flashing signal that we are stumbling when we should be soaring.

Think of it this way: The apostle Paul said believers are "jars of clay," vessels into which God's Spirit can be poured. Shame tells us clay pots that we have developed a crack and sprung a leak. Thankfully, God is a master craftsman skilled at patching up broken jars and putting them to good use.

SOME SHAME IS UNDESERVED AND HARMFUL

Human emotions easily get tangled and twisted. If we could X-ray our feelings, they would probably look like a huge bowl of spaghetti or a fifty-car pileup on the highway. Since our emotions are rarely neat and tidy, it's not surprising that lots of people feel unreasonable shame. In these cases, a healthy sense of shame is distorted, exaggerated, and leads to false beliefs.

Unjustified shame comes from many sources:

Our Culture

Sometimes it's our society's warped perspective of what gives a person value and worth. What does our culture tell us? You *matter* only if you're good-looking, popular, wealthy, influential, and talented. In ten thousand ways every day, our media-saturated society communicates that we are defective and deficient if we aren't a superstar or a supermodel. Our culture heaps on the shame if we are too fat or too thin, too poor or too powerless, too bland or too boring.

Our Beliefs

For people of faith, shame sometimes comes from legalistic and perfectionistic church communities. A church lacking a proper understanding of grace tells us that, to be worthwhile, we must conform to certain standards and comply with certain expectations. We must attend to the "do's" and avoid the "don'ts." When we believe our worth is measured by *what we do* rather than *who we are*, we're sure to feel rotten. We'll never be able to do enough and be enough. Grace-less religion creates the illusion that if we only follow the letter of the law, we will be acceptable; if we fail, we will be rejected and despised. But this is the opposite of the gospel of Christ.

Our Parents

Other times our parents leave us feeling shamed. Moms and dads sometimes communicate, verbally or nonverbally, that their children don't measure up, fall short of expectations, are more trouble than they're worth. If parents put conditions on acceptability (good grades, sports trophies, gold stars in Sunday school), the child will end up feeling fundamentally flawed. Even devoted, well-meaning parents sometimes unknowingly saddle their kids with unintended shame, leaving them to bear the heavy burden of inferiority and inadequacy.

Ourself

Perhaps the most powerful source of shame is within ourselves. Even if the rest of the world tells us we are okay, accepted, and forgiven, we don't believe it and keep on bathing in the deep pool of shame we've dug for ourselves. I've met with countless people during my pastoral ministry who tell me they cannot get out from underneath their own guilt. I explain to them the forgiveness of God through Christ, and they still can't find freedom.

I challenge them by saying, "Do you think you are bigger than God?" They always look at me surprised and reply, "No." Then if you believe He is bigger, and if He has already forgiven you, why are you not forgiving yourself? They usually just reply with something like, *I can't. I'm too ashamed.*

"Oh, I see," I gently yet pointedly reply, "your shame makes you bigger than God." To which they quickly retort with something like, "Well, no . . . God is bigger than me and my shame!" With that, I just ask them to repeat that statement again. After they hear themselves say it once more, I say, "Exactly!" A small view of God will always keep us in the confines of our guilt.

All four shame-inflictors take the image of God created within us, and the forgiveness we can have in Christ, and try to replace them with the goal of a false image impossible to achieve. If we accept the image of the self we think or have been told we should attain, we feel ashamed if we don't hit the target. This kind of shame is not what God created in the first Adam, nor is it what He gave us in the second Adam, Jesus Christ. You see, Christ came to do away with sin and the guilt and shame that come with it. We needed a second Adam because the first Adam blew it. If we continue to live in shame, we are remaining in the way of the first Adam, who was separated from God after the fall by a great canyon of sin and shame. But if we accept the Second Adam, our shame is taken away (Romans 8:1) and we gain freedom in Christ (Romans 8:2).

SHAME DRIVES US TO HIDE FROM GOD

In chapter 3, we discussed how Adam and Eve sinned against God and then went into hiding—or tried to. When God came looking for them in the garden, they hid among the trees. God asked why, and Adam answered, "I heard the sound of you in the garden, and I was afraid, because I was naked, and I hid myself" (Genesis 3:10). Ashamed, Adam and Eve tried to avoid God. This began a pattern that continues to this day: when we feel like we've blown it, our first impulse is usually to run *from* God, not *to* Him.

The problem comes when we feel shame because of wrongdoing or wrong thinking—some perpetual sin we can't seem to beat—and we fail to be honest with God. We stay on the surface, fearing the skeletons in the closet we're hoping He won't find. This is where our "spiritual schizophrenia" kicks in: we know intellectually God is already aware of our ill intentions and misdeeds, but we still want to keep them hidden from Him. The longer we remain in our sin, the stronger our inclination to run and hide from God. Staying in a shameful place only drives a wedge deeper between us and Him. The wedge is only there because we put it there; He never leaves us or forsakes us.

SHAME CAN BE HEALED AND ERASED

If this topic has touched a painful nerve, let me give you a dose of strong anesthetic. God never intended us to stay mired in muck; He doesn't want our dirty dishes stashed in the shower. He certainly never wants us to experience unhealthy shame, and He wants us to seek healing for our justified shame fully and quickly so we can move forward in growth. The good news is that shame can be wiped away. The healing of our shameful feelings begins with a spiritual encounter—specifically, a profound experience of God's amazing grace and unfailing love.

Much of this book is intended to show how God wants to remove roadblocks in our lives, including shame, so we can draw close to Him in honesty and intimacy. For now, let me offer a cup of cool water as we journey forward. King David, the man after God's own heart who also tasted agonizing shame, wrote: "I sought the Lord, and he answered me and delivered me from all my fears. Those who look to him are radiant, and their faces shall never be ashamed. . . . The Lord is near to the brokenhearted and saves the crushed in spirit" (Psalm 34:4–5, 18). Scripture promises that if we humbly seek God and confess our sins, He will wipe away our guilt and shame—forever.

There's more. If you stagger through life under the burdensome weight of shame, remember the words of Jesus: "Come to me, all who labor and are heavy laden, and I will give you rest. Take my yoke upon you, and learn from me, for I am gentle and lowly in heart, and you will find rest for your souls. For my yoke is easy, and my burden is light" (Matthew 11:28–30). Your shame can be the noose you hang by, or the rope you use to pull yourself closer to God's grace. This begins with a conscious decision to not run but to "come to Me." Jesus invites people weighed down by shame to exchange their heaviness for His lightness.

So come on, let's find some rest from the burdens we carry. He promises to be gentle; there is no reason to hesitate. The more vulnerable we get, the more of His grace we'll experience (James 4:6).

PART TWO

ROADBLOCKS TO
HONESTY WITH GOD

CHAPTER 6

DECEIVING OURSELVES

TRUTH IS THE DEATH SENTENCE FOR THE FAKE YOU

A college student named Connor confided to me over late-night lattes, "My girlfriend found out I've been looking at porn on-line, and she blew a gasket. But c'mon—it's not like I'm the only guy who checks out porn. It's everywhere."

Sonia is a divorced single mother facing foreclosure on her home. Why? Because she's racked up so much debt buying stuff she didn't need that she's now buried under the weight of all the bills.

Neil told me recently his marriage is on thin ice, ready to cave in. His wife of fourteen years got fed up with being a "married widow," as she called it, lonely and isolated, while he ran his software business, traveled the country for meetings, and spent weekends doing paperwork.

Then there's Stacey, a standout high school senior who's got the world by the tail. She's a cheerleader, honor roll student, award-winning swimmer, and leader in her church group. She also has woefully, and inexplicably, low self-esteem. Despite overwhelming evidence to the contrary, she believes she'll never measure up or amount to anything.

The details of the stories may not seem alike on the surface. But in fact there is one striking commonality: All of these individuals, in their own way, are deceiving themselves. Their self-deception has led them to believe falsehoods and do unhealthy things. The lens through which they view themselves and others is distorted, warping their perceptions. But they don't realize it. We all are like this, oftentimes in very subtle, inconspicuous ways. To not see *truly* is in some ways to not see at all, and we are easily blinded by our own false realities.

Self-deception is a process of denying, justifying, or rationalizing away truths or facts. It's a subconscious means of keeping ourselves in the dark, oblivious to a falsehood or contradiction within us. Without even thinking about it, we hide from our own awareness of what is inconsistent and incongruent.

You see it in the alcoholic who insists he doesn't have a problem and can stop drinking any time he wants. You see it in the parents who are sure their daughter, the apple of their eye, is not sexually promiscuous—despite the checklist of signs that say she is. You see it in the student who cheats on all her college exams but shrugs it off with an *everyone-does-it* attitude. You see it in the extremely likable guy, constantly striving to earn acceptance and please everyone.

The issue of self-deception has been around a long, long time. The Greek philosopher Plato, regarded as one of the wisest people ever, asserted, "The worst of all deceptions is self-deception." Shakespeare, in his play *Hamlet*, wrote, "This above all: To thine own self be true." It's a recurring theme in the Bible too. The prophet Jeremiah pointed out that the heart is deceitful above all things and asked, "Who can understand it?" (17:9). Paul wrote to the Galatian believers, "If anyone thinks he is something, when he is nothing, he deceives himself" (6:3). John said, "If we say we have no sin, we deceive ourselves, and the truth is not in us" (1 John 1:8).

If we're not honest with ourselves—about who we are, why we do what we do, what lurks within our hearts—then we're incapable of addressing issues that hold us back. We're incapable of knowing what drives us, motivates us, and compels us. We're incapable of detecting what's broken and needs to be fixed. And we're incapable of seeing reality *truly*, which really means we're blind.

Here's the bottom line about self-deception as it relates to our quest for authenticity with God:

We can't be honest with God if we aren't honest with ourselves.

We can't tell Him our deepest struggles, admit our failings, or seek help for our most vexing problems if we don't acknowledge them to ourselves first. Similarly, we can't celebrate our victories and experience joy in God's presence if we have an inaccurate image of whom He created us to be. Whatever our area of self-deception, it prevents us from being fully, down-to-the-core real with our Father. And anything less than that is less than the close-knit, intimate relationship God invites us to enjoy with Him.

WHO AM I FOOLING?

Several years ago I appeared on the national radio broadcast *Focus on the Family* to discuss my book *Dad, If You Only Knew*. I had lots I wanted to say and felt privileged to be on the program. But as I sat there being interviewed, knowing millions of people were listening, I couldn't help but feel insignificant, even incompetent. Nonetheless, I tried hard to be as articulate and authentic as I could.

After the show, I began talking with the cohost Juli Slattery, who is a trained psychologist. At one point she said, "Good job on the broadcast, Josh." I immediately brushed aside the compliment and started listing all the things I thought I'd done wrong. I could've delivered the message more clearly, I forgot a key point, I muddled a story—on and on.

Finally, Juli held up a hand to stop me. "Josh, have you ever heard of the Imposter Syndrome?"

With that question, I felt as if I were laid bare on the exam table and she, the doctor, had just discovered a tumor growing in a hidden place in my body. With those few words, I knew she had diagnosed an issue I'd struggled with forever, but had never stopped long enough to realize was a problem.

She went on to explain. "The Imposter Syndrome is an issue for competent, accomplished people consumed with insecurity and self-doubt. They're convinced they don't deserve their success and think it's just a matter of time before they're exposed as frauds. Real achievements and successes are dismissed as luck, good timing, or a fluke." Then she said, "Ring any bells, Josh?"

Yeah, like Big Ben gonging in my head. She was right. I saw myself as a fraud, as one big walking lie. Who am I to speak in front of crowds, write books, be on the radio, pastor a church? At any moment, some authority—probably an older gentleman in a serious Brooks Brothers suit, round spectacles, and a nasally voice—was going to barge in and tell me to go sit down like a good little boy.

My self-deception was this: I believed I wasn't good enough, that I didn't have the right stuff to do what I was doing. I thought God should be using somebody else, somebody better, somebody who actually knew what he was talking about. For a long time I rode the woe-is-me train all the way to I'm-a-Loserville. Believe me, I've bought the ticket on this locomotive more often than I'd like to admit.

But the strange thing was I never expressed this to God. In fact, God is probably the one I felt most like an imposter in front of. He knew the real me, along with all my shortcomings. In fear of actually ever talking about them, I prayed surface prayers, stayed on safe topics, and avoided acknowledging my self-doubts. The more success I had, the more I felt like an imposter. How could God know the sins I'm struggling with and still give me so many great opportunities? Imposter! Herein lies the single greatest hindrance to honesty with God—myself. But I never want to admit that. Self-deprecation and low self-esteem is a form of pride as well. Eeyore of Winnie the Pooh was one of the most self-absorbed characters to ever hit the screen. Even when we wallow in our shortcomings, we are selfishly thinking about nothing else but ourselves. Yet we never really think of this as pride; we only think of pride as being too confident in our own talents.

LEGGO MY EGO

It's pretty easy to sniff out someone else's self-absorption because it's obnoxious and off-putting. Sometimes we refer to these people as narcissistic, named for the character in Greek mythology who fell in love with his own reflection and died because he couldn't pull himself away.

Our history books are full of people whose inflated egos drove them to build empires or destroy them, amass fortunes or squander them. I am fascinated by one of the all-time greatest narcissists, whose story is told in the Old Testament book of Daniel. King Nebuchadnezzar, strong-arm ruler of Babylon, held power over a huge country and enjoyed vast wealth. One evening on his palace roof, he looked across the greatest city of the ancient world and proclaimed, "Is not this the great Babylon I have built as the royal residence, by my mighty power and for the glory of my majesty?" Enamored with his own reflection, so to speak, he created a golden idol for himself and ordered all the people to bow and worship before it.

Still, he was a man humbled by God more than once. He'd been given firm warnings in his dreams, interpreted by Daniel, that his kingdom was going to crumble and he was not as big of a big shot as he imagined. God wanted Nebuchadnezzar to know that He placed earthly kings on their thrones and that He was the ultimate King. Nonetheless, he continued to live a life of pride. It wasn't until his ultimate humiliation, when God turned him into a man-animal and he was forced to eat grass and live among wild beasts for seven years, that he finally praised God.

We may not be tyrannical, egomaniacal rulers, but each of us has our own little fiefdom, our own little world of influence and control. We can be selfish and self-centered without being aware of it. Even people who wouldn't be categorized as full-blown narcissists can still deceive themselves into thinking they're superior to others. Psychologists call this the state of "illusory superiority." It's also called the "Lake Wobegone Effect," from Garrison Keillor's fictional Minnesota town where "all the children are above average." It simply means we tend to inflate our positive qualities and abilities, especially in comparison to other people. Christian Psychologist Dr. Mark McMinn contends that the "Lake Wobegone Effect" is fueled by pride. "One of the clearest conclusions of social science research is that we are proud," he says. "We think better of ourselves than we really are, we see our faults in faint black and white rather than in vivid color, and we assume the worst in others while assuming the best in ourselves."* We may not be aware of our self-deprecating self-absorption, noxious narcissism or superiority complex, but it's there. And it's a roadblock to real relationships. Especially the one we have with God. Why? Because pride is the root of all sin. Think about it—everything we do that is sinful has a selfish side to it. Therefore, whatever form pride takes in our life throws us into a sinful and selfish state before God and hinders our intimacy with Him. Sadly, we don't often see this until it is pointed out to us.

* Mark McMinn, *Why Sin Matters* (Carol Stream, IL: Tyndale, 2004), 69–71.

SEEING YOUR BLIND SPOTS

I love the story told by renowned neurologist Oliver Sacks in his book *An Anthropologist on Mars*. A patient of his named Virgil had been blind since early childhood. When he was fifty years old, he underwent surgery to restore his eyesight. But as Virgil and Dr. Sacks discovered, possessing physical eyesight is not the same as *seeing*.

"Virgil's first experiences with sight were confusing. He was able to make out colors and movements, but arranging them into a coherent picture was more difficult. Over time he learned to identify various objects, but his habits—his behaviors—were still those of a blind man."

Dr. Sacks concluded, "One must die as a blind person to be born again as a seeing person."*

All of us are "blind" to some degree. We are unaware of certain aspects of ourselves, and it can be hard to see the truth through our preconceived ideas. Emotional and spiritual blind spots keep us from seeing ourselves clearly and then trick us into believing in a reality that may not be true.

The problem with blind spots is that—you got it—we're blind to them. We can't see our areas of weakness. So how do we go about being "born again" as a seeing person? Once you have been saved by the gospel of Jesus Christ, there's no magical formula for moving from self-deception to self-awareness, but let me give you a crash course from the lessons I've learned about seeing yourself clearly.

Ask for God's Spirit to open your mind. Paul prayed that God would give his fellow believers "the Spirit of wisdom and revelation, so that you may know him better. I pray also that the eyes of your heart may be enlightened" (Ephesians 1:17–18 NIV). Make this a prayer for yourself, that the Spirit would turn on the floodlights in your head and heart.

* Terry Seufferlein, SermonIllustrations.com, http://www.sermonillustrations.com/a-z/b/blindness.htm.

Be quiet and listen. We live in a noisy world, where dozens of things vie for our attention—emails, beeping cell phones, TVs, and on and on. I wonder how many times God tries to get through to us only to get our voice mail. If you want to hear from Him, set aside time to listen for His still, small voice. Start your day in stillness, before the world starts clanging and banging, and read God's Word with an attentive heart. Take ten minutes to pray in your car before heading off to work. Go to the local coffee shop, like I do, early in the morning to get away from your warm bed and sit in a lit cafe to meet with God. Turn off your gadgets and gizmos for a day and be attuned to what God wants to tell you about yourself and Himself.

Take inventory. It's no surprise that one of the first steps in twelve-step programs for addictions is to take a detailed personal inventory of your life. Whether or not you're dealing with an addiction or a dependence problem, this is a helpful step for *everyone*. Taking inventory means leaving no stone unturned and refusing to shy away from tough questions. Whom have you hurt? What regrets do you have? Do you like yourself? What makes you laugh? What makes you cry? Where have you neglected the gospel of Christ in your life? There are dozens of books and online sources to assist you in this process of intentional evaluation. Some of the Puritan believers of old understood the power of this activity and have left us wonderful writings to assist in Christ-centered contemplation (see John Owen, for example). Maybe the best place to start is by grabbing a journal and sitting still somewhere for an hour, asking God to help you begin the stone-flipping process in your own life.

Enlist allies in your quest. We all need trusted friends or mentors to hold up a mirror to us. Other people can often see us more clearly than we can see ourselves. Ask for open and honest feedback from people you trust. It will take courage; it will mean being vulnerable. But this is how awareness occurs. When you've found a trustworthy friend or family member, ask, "Do you see anything in me, positive or negative, that I might not see in myself? What do I need to work on? What rough edges need smoothing? Where have I lost sight of God in my life?"

Journal every day. You don't need to write for more than ten or fifteen minutes, but it's critical that you record your honest thoughts and feelings as they come to you. I have a small journal I write in every day, at least one page a day. The goal is to tap into my internal reservoir and bring out what needs to be exposed for the sake of change. A few nights ago I sat with my stack of journals, a cup of coffee, and my wife, and we read through the things I've written over the years. Some of these things were hilarious while others were humiliating. Nonetheless, I was able to see the things God revealed to me and the way He has changed me from year to year.

For example, we found a period of my life where I was struggling with purity. It seems like I quoted Psalm 51 on every other page. In all my begging and pleading for cleansing and strength, I was able to see the way God was working on my heart to uproot ungodliness so that I could have more of His holiness.

Some pages captured my frustration over manipulative bosses, empty bank accounts, family feuds, and abandoned dreams. My wife laughed hysterically over an entire entry dedicated to my "sixteen overdraft fees" from the bank. Even in my poorest and most broken moments, as well as on my greatest days, I could see the way God brought His Word to my mind as a means of conforming me to His will. My journals serve as a chronicle of my journey to authentic living before God and dependence on Him daily.

Talk with a counselor or pastor. Counseling isn't only for crisis management and tackling tough issues; it's also an excellent resource for self-discovery. Schedule several meetings to explore what's really going on inside you. Some of my most enlightening hours have been spent with biblical counselors who have helped me see what I can't see myself.

If you want to see God more clearly, stop deceiving yourself. Christ didn't die to save your image, He died to save *you*. So whatever your inner imposter is, kill him off—He may be the very thing keeping you from knowing God more intimately.

CHAPTER 7

POLISHED PRETENDERS

HYPOCRISY UNDERMINES SPIRITUAL HONESTY

High on my list of thought-provoking films is *Catch Me If You Can*, the 2002 motion picture about con man extraordinaire Frank Abagnale Jr. The tagline called the movie "The true story of a real fake." As the films opens, we learn that in 1963 Frank (played by Leonardo DiCaprio) is sixteen years old and living with his parents in New Rochelle, New York. Trouble brews when a bank refuses to give his dad a business loan because of tax issues, and the family must move from their spacious house into a cramped apartment. Worse, Frank's mother is having an affair with a friend of her husband.

Frank's first foray into public deception comes when he poses as a substitute teacher in his high school French class. That's just the beginning. Devastated by his parents' divorce, Frank leaves home. It isn't long before he runs out of money and begins to swindle people, discovering he's got a knack for the art of deception. Soon his cons grow more audacious: he impersonates an airline pilot and forges Pan Am payroll checks worth more than $2.8 million.

Enter FBI agent Carl Hanratty (Tom Hanks), who begins to track Frank's activities. Eventually, Carl and Frank meet in a hotel, where Frank convinces Carl he's Secret Service. Later, at Christmas, Frank calls to apologize for duping him.

Despite being chased by the FBI, Frank goes on to impersonate a doctor and a lawyer, his charades so skillful that he convinces even professionals in the fields. He also falls in love with Brenda, one of the few people he admits the truth to about his fraudulent acts. After a series of close calls with Carl, check forgery all over Western Europe, more scams and escapes, the truth (and the law) catches up with Frank. He's apprehended and sentenced to twelve years in prison, receiving occasional visits from Carl. In the end, Carl persuades his superiors to cut a deal so Frank can serve the remainder of his sentence working for the bank fraud department of the FBI.

A written message prior to the credits reveals that Frank has been happily married for twenty-six years and has three sons. Still friends with Carl, Frank has helped to catch some of the world's most elusive forgers.

MAY I BE FRANK WITH YOU?

I'm the kind of guy who thinks about a movie for days or weeks after watching it, mulling it over in my mind, pondering the plot, characters, and themes. After watching *Catch Me If You Can* initially, and a few times since, I've examined my own life to see if I'm just another Frank Abagnale Jr. Do I set out to deceive people by adopting a persona? Do I pretend to be something I'm not to gain an advantage? Certainly, I don't do it with malicious or criminal intent, but at times I've felt I have kept up fronts to get what I want, earn admiration from others, or win pats on the back.

I'm not alone in this. In fact, I've come to believe there's a little bit of Frank Abagnale Jr. in all of us—for some people, there's *a lot*. Not that we're skilled scam artists, probably not even petty thieves for that matter. No, I mean our tendency to put on "masks" and cultivate a gussied-up guise to fool people into believing we're the person we want to be, not the person we actually are. We don't perpetrate fraud, assume false names, or display fake IDs; our trickery is far more subtle. So subtle, in fact, that we might not be aware we're doing it. We withhold the full truth about ourselves, and in doing so, create an ever-so-slightly airbrushed, altered version of our real selves.

You know exactly what I mean if you've ever been at church and kept a sweet smile plastered on even though you felt pretty miserable . . . or overstated your success to impress someone . . . or glossed over the less tidy aspects of yourself . . . or pretended everything is A-OK instead of admitting your pain and hurt.

I admit I'm frequently tempted to act the way others want me to and align my beliefs according to some predetermined checklist. Like a chameleon, I can change colors to better blend in. Or like the lemming, I might follow the crowd so no one thinks I'm different or weird.

You too? We know what authenticity demands: To be completely ourselves, to be forthright about our beliefs, and to behave in a way that's in sync with who we are at our core. There is no falsehood or facade, no hedging or hiding. In the words of that esteemed philosopher Popeye, "I yam what I yam"—and I'm nót afraid to show what *I yam* to the world.

Toward the end of *Catch Me If You Can*, Frank makes one last attempt to run by impersonating a pilot again. Carl catches up with him at Dulles Airport and walks several paces behind. The FBI agent warns Frank that if he keeps running, he's going to get caught and likely spend his life in prison. Besides, Carl tells him, he spent four years trying to arrange his release, convincing the FBI and the US Attorney General that Frank wouldn't run. Frank is actually surprised to see Carl, because Carl was supposed to be out of town, visiting his ostensibly young daughter, who is away on a ski trip.

Frank: You said your daughter was four years old. You're lying.

Carl: She was four when I left. Now she's fifteen. My wife's been remarried for eleven years. I see Grace every now and again.

Frank: I don't understand.

Carl: Sure you do. Sometimes it's easier living the lie.[*]

Most of us would not cop to "living the lie"—we don't intentionally and willfully tell untruths. But it is, for many of us, easier to polish our image and maintain a facade than to let others see us as we really are, flaws, faults, and all. We act differently around different people, carefully manage our image to make a good impression, and conceal parts of ourselves that might cause people to think less of us.

But wait, you say, nearly everyone presents an image to the world. That's life in the twenty-first century. Plastic surgeons can cut off our flaws, we can Photoshop out our wrinkles, we can shine up our Facebook profile page, and can enhance our resume. Can we expect any different? And really, what's the big deal?

The big deal is this: **when we aren't real with other people, we form a habit of phoniness that spills over into our relationship with God**. It's nearly impossible to "flip a switch" from being *fake with people* to being *real with God*. Pretense with other human beings often leads to pretense with our heavenly Father. Therefore, if we're serious about learning to be honest with God, we'll strive to develop *authenticity as a way of life*, in every relationship.

Since we all feel tremendous pressure to pretend and prevaricate, it's important to understand where that pressure comes from. Here are three of the top sources.

---

[*] *Catch Me If You Can*, directed by Steven Spielberg (Dreamworks SKG, 2002).

Cultural Conditioning

Do you remember the familiar slogan of the '90s, "Image Is Everything"? That catchphrase was made famous by an advertisement for Canon cameras featuring tennis star Andre Agassi, who at the time was notorious for his bad-boy reputation. The commercials seemed to air constantly and the tagline became ubiquitous, seen on billboards and emblazoned on T-shirts. Despite criticism that the ad promoted style over substance, the message became woven into our country's lexicon and, I believe, embedded in its collective consciousness.

In the years since, the "Image Is Everything" sentiment seems to have only increased in scope and intensity. Among the many wonderful qualities of our society, here's one that's not so great: We are largely superficial and shallow, simulated and synthetic. We have highly skilled and highly paid people who serve as "image consultants" and "spin doctors." Advertisers convince us that a certain product will make us more appealing and attractive. Politicians are packaged, with agendas they *sell* to the public. Even so-called reality shows on TV are staged, orchestrated, and manipulated.

Nowadays, it's hard to imagine life without online access, but this too can condition us to be image-conscious. Years ago when Facebook first started, I didn't want to join, assuming it was one of those seemingly faddish websites sweeping college campuses. Eventually, my sister convinced me to register. She was sure it would be the key to keeping our communication intact over the thousand miles that separated us. Now it seems half the world is on Facebook, or other social networking sites. But I wonder: Is this whole online personality thing really just a better way to communicate with our friends, or are we seeking to validate our existence by constructing an impressive profile page? Is this just a convenient way to bolster our image and make our friends, distant acquaintances, and people we talked with once or twice think we're hip, clever, and successful?

I don't mean this as a diatribe against popular culture. There's much to be enjoyed and appreciated, especially for those of us blessed with freedom and opportunity. But we have to admit that shallowness and superficiality pervade our society. It is extremely difficult to "be in the world, but not of the world."

Penchant for People-Pleasing

Do I want people to like me? Of course I do! And so do you. There's nothing wrong with wanting to please others. We're all wired with the desire for affirmation and approval from other people, especially those most important to us. God created us with a deep-down drive to be highly regarded by those around us.

The problem comes when we look to someone else to decide whether we're valuable and worthy. When we believe that being liked and appreciated is the way to be a worthwhile human being, our people pleasing becomes unhealthy and destructive. That's because being truthful and authentic means we won't please all of the people all of the time. In fact, being honest about ourselves carries the risk that some may not like what they see and hear. They may be disappointed and disillusioned with us. Jesus told His followers, "There's trouble ahead when you live only for the approval of others, saying what flatters them, doing what indulges them. Popularity contests are not truth contests. . . . Your task is to be true, not popular" (Luke 6:26 THE MESSAGE).

We must give up the idea that we are loveable, good, and worthy only if other people say we are. We have all believed that at one time or another; some of us believe it all the time. But it doesn't work. When you always try to meet other people's standards, you will likely overlook the one thing you're called to do on this earth—to be the individual God created you to be.

If our worth and value aren't determined by other people, how is it determined? Through our relationship with God, our Creator, Father, friend. Christ died to establish—to stitch into the fabric of reality—this truth: *You are loved—period. You are a child of the King. No strings attached.* We must come to believe, without a shred of doubt, the words of Paul: nothing can ever separate us from His love (Romans 8:38–39).

It's Easier to Fake It Than Make It

Being real takes more effort, energy, and persistence than merely projecting an image. It's easier to purchase a degree online for $29.95 to hang on your wall than spend years actually going to class and writing papers. It's easier to get liposuction or take steroids than to be disciplined to show up at the gym for a few hours each week. It's easier to put a fish sticker on the back of your car than make Christ the center of your life.

Of course, issues of character are far more important. It takes much more diligence and self-discipline to *be* holy than to merely *act* holy. But plenty of people have discovered it's easier to look good rather than be good. They choose style over substance, appearance over authenticity. This isn't just a modern-day issue, it's been going on for centuries. In His day, Jesus had strong words for people who created an outward show of righteousness without developing the inward virtues.

Not one to put up with duplicity, Jesus firmly and forcefully addressed this problem, pointing out that transformation comes from the inside out. Addressing the Pharisees and other hypocritical religious leaders, He said, "Woe to you, scribes and Pharisees, hypocrites! For you are like whitewashed tombs, which outwardly appear beautiful, but within are full of dead people's bones and all uncleanness. So you also outwardly appear righteous to others, but within you are full of hypocrisy and lawlessness" (Matthew 23:27–28).

In Jesus' day, tombs were painted white on the outside so they would appear attractive. But inside was the stinky, rotting flesh of dead bodies. All of Jesus' listeners would have understood what He meant—a person's exterior can look impressive while the interior is filthy and corrupt. We might read this passage and think the message was only for the holier-than-thou hypocrites who misled people in biblical times. But this is just as much a warning to you and me. Let's take a good, hard look at our own lives to see if we are seeking to become holy and pure vessels for God's use—or merely settling for a fancy but phony facade.

Rather than focusing on our image, we should focus on our heart instead. Since only good things spring from a pure heart, we won't need to worry about how we come across to people. By focusing on the inside, we follow God's example: "For the Lord sees not as man sees: man looks on the outward appearance, but the Lord looks on the heart" (1 Samuel 16:7).

MAKING MY MAGIC ACT DISAPPEAR

As a boy, I was known as "Alexander the Great." All my friends, family, and classmates called me Josh, but audiences who came to see me perform magic shows knew me by my stage name (which I adopted in honor of my grandfather, who was a world-renowned magician). For many years, magic was a huge part of my life, and I practiced several hours a day to perfect my tricks and stagecraft. From age eight to fifteen, I performed dozens of times each year at churches, talent shows, Halloween alternative events, and birthday parties.

Around age ten, I was given my favorite "magic shirt" as a birthday gift. A navy blue silk shirt, it looked extra magical to me, and I wore it for almost all my shows. Before I got that shimmery shirt, I dressed in a suit and tie, and my mom would pin a little red rose on my lapel. The flower was silk, not real, but it looked dapper. Just in case, I always carried a clown outfit to parties if they needed a clown instead of a magician.

There's a reason I'm sharing this journey down memory lane. Magic, as you know, is all about illusion, deception, sleight of hand, misdirection. It's about convincing people they're seeing something they're not, or not seeing something that's there. The magician has to *sell* the trick; to do so, he has to sell himself as a smooth, believable, and persuasive performer.

I can't help but draw parallels between my skill as a young magician, who fooled otherwise astute people, and the grown-up me, who fools otherwise astute people. I was, and am, a master of illusion. I gave up performing magic when one of our family dogs killed my rabbit, Elvis Parsley, who was an amazing, trained "partner" in my act. Devastated at his untimely passing, I couldn't go on. So I boxed up my top hat, magic wand, and tons of props, and put them in the garage. My career as the "Kid Magician" had reached its finale. Curtain closed.

That was then, this is now. As a grown man I'm also trying to stop being a master illusionist with my life. Getting people to "suspend disbelief" is fun and exciting when everyone knows it's all an act; it's not fun or exciting in the nitty-gritty of real life. The apostle Paul said that when he was a child he thought as a child, but when he became a man he put away childish things (1 Corinthians 13:11). Spiritual maturity means letting go of misguided actions and attitudes and moving on to those that are trustworthy and holy. It's a process, to be sure. In recent years I've tried hard to put away my inclination to make people think I'm something I'm not. I'm trying to leave behind the pretense and posturing, and just be me—with God and other people. No tricks, no illusions.

Want to join me?

CHAPTER 8

IMAGE MANAGEMENT

FINDING FREEDOM FROM A TWO-FACED FAITH

On the first warm day of spring in Colorado, I sat in a high school class—much to my dismay—listening to a guest speaker. I struggled to keep my eyelids open. Before the guest was able to get through half of her talk, our assistant principal abruptly came into the room. With tears in his eyes and anguish on his face, he said, "There's been a shooting at Columbine." I felt like my heart stopped as my mind raced.

I was seated just four or five miles from Columbine High School. I am not sure I had prayed or even thought about God that morning, but by the afternoon, faith and prayer were all I had to hold on to. The next day, April 21, I stood on the other side of the yellow police tape near Columbine and asked God to make Himself clear. *Why God? Why now? Why here, in our hometown? Where are You?*

Three students joined me in prayer along with three other students—one who attended Columbine and ran for his life the day before, and two others from another Littleton school—like me, shaken by the tragedy. That day after the shooting, we did more than forty TV interviews that started soon after we finished praying that morning. With every interview, I gave an account for my hope in God, all the while saying something in the back of my mind like, *God, You better show up and prove Yourself here or we're all going to look like idiots.*

At about two o'clock in the afternoon, a short, stout man from the *St. Louis News* interviewed me. At the same time, my friend Craig was being interviewed by MTV a few yards from me. During the interview, I noticed out of the corner of my eye that Craig was suddenly weeping between questions. Prior to that interview, Craig had just found out he had lost his friend Cassie in the shooting. I asked the crew interviewing me to turn off the camera, and I ran and held Craig. Justin and Sean came over too and we all huddled together, cried and prayed for about twenty minutes. Then we began to sing.

As we sang worship songs to God, I began to hear many other voices. I looked up to find that almost all of the people in the park had gathered around our circle. They were singing with us, even those who did not know the words. They just wanted in on the hope we had found. In that profound moment, when a circle of four guys grew to a huddle of a hundred-plus, God made it clear: He had been there the whole time.

Overwhelmed with emotion and the feeling of His presence, I cried out, *"God, if there is anyone in this circle who does not know You, may they cry out to You right now!"* Then I heard the most beautiful sound I've ever heard in my life—voices, many voices, began calling out to God. At that moment, only yards from the Columbine campus, the tragedy became triumph. It was no longer a day of death but of life. It had seemed God was nowhere to be found, but He was just waiting for us to return to Him the whole time.

It's almost embarrassing to think that earlier that day I was worried about how I would look—or how God would look—before all the media, while God was caring about something deeper. God just wanted me to run to Him in faith.

HIDING FROM WHO KNOWS WHAT

Why do we wander away in the first place? What causes us to either doubt or become distracted to the point of leaving the God we claim to love?

We have a problem deep down, all the way to our roots. Each of us possesses a sin nature, a soul DNA of dishonesty with God. We find ourselves miles from home because of our lack of alignment with who God is and what He says about us. It starts with a wrong view of God and results in a wrong view of self.

You see, in the same way we manage our image with people, we can make a career out of managing an image before God. We have a version of ourselves we think He'd like to see—or simply the one we want Him to see—so we work hard to maintain it. All the while we keep ourselves blind to seeing who God really is—removed from the reality that God knows all and sees all. Here are a few ways we hide from God (I know because, sadly, I've done them).

• *Halfhearted thankfulness.* We pray casual, semiartificial prayers like, "Thank You for this food" or "Thank You for this day" or "Thanks for Your blessings." While these are not bad prayers, they often are uttered without much thought, quickly dispensed so we can dig in to the plate in front of us or because we're worried how we look in the restaurant with head bowed and eyes closed (especially if we're holding hands). Too often this is the only kind of prayer we say throughout the day, never truly taking time to be honest with God. Our less-than-passionate prayers of gratefulness are done out of routine, a means to maintain the image of appreciation in hopes that God will keep the good stuff coming.

• *Affirming our usefulness.* Like a child who seeks the approval of her father, we go on doing good things for people so God will be proud. We let the star system of our Sunday school days bleed over into our adult faith, believing that every time we do something good (even as simple as bringing our Bible to church) that God is giving us a gold star in heaven. We try to prove to God we're doing so much for Him and are therefore *useful.* Though we denounce a salvation based on achievements, we go on trying to achieve so we can earn something or keep something we've earned. Lots of believers turn themselves from joyful bond servants to grumbling slaves. It's as if we say, "See how much I do for You, God? I'm indispensible."

• *Pseudo-scholars.* "Look what I found in Your Word, God!" we declare to God, as if He is going to give us valedictorian status because of our intellect. Pockets of believers approach God's Word as an academic exercise rather than a means to grow in greater faith in God. They fall more in love with knowing *about* God than knowing God personally. They preach, write, speak, present, or casually converse in a way with other Christians to show off their deep insights into theology or Scripture, all the while hoping God is seeing how insightful they are. Sure, there is great value in studying Scripture and theology, but it still must be God we try to find and not just knowledge so we can look like the smartest kid in the class, and impressive to the Lord.

• *Continuously contrite.* There have been periods of my life where God has heard nothing more from me than "Help!" or "I blew it" or "I'm sorry." Sometimes our communication with God is all about the big mess we're in and how sorry we are to be there. Genuine contrition and sorrow for our failures brings us closer to God; groveling and cringing before Him endlessly can be a mask we wear. Some people remain continuously apologetic, assuming that's what He wants to hear. We keep up the image of the "sorrowful servant" or "weeping prophet" without real desire to change. If we continue in sin, assuaging our guilt with more apologies, we are no longer really affected by the weight of the guilt. Our "I'm sorry" becomes nothing more than empty words that we believe God wants to hear.

• *Wallowing in worthlessness.* When all else fails, we totally remove ourselves from God, believing we are doing Him a favor. We uphold an image that we are disgraceful and not worth anything to Him. We mark ourselves with a big black *X* spiritually, trying to quarantine ourselves from God and His people. We portray ourselves as dirty, sick, unholy, or sacrilegious because we think that is what God sees and is how we should see ourselves. Even if we know deep down that His grace is big enough for all our mistakes, we take this image on as a way of avoiding God and being real with Him.

These are images we cultivate and cling to far too often. And you know what? Every one of them stems from possessing a limited, small view of God. We think He is just another version of us, easily appeased by an outward expression that keeps the inside hidden. This couldn't be further from the truth. We are told in Galatians 6:7, "Do not be deceived: God is not mocked." We could go on fooling ourselves and thinking we are convincing someone with the image we're portraying before the Lord, but the Bible says flat out, "Don't be naïve! Don't play games with God!" He sees and knows everything, and you can't fool Him. He doesn't hide but waits for you to be real with Him.

HIDE, SEEK, AND SCARE

When I was eight or nine, my siblings and I played a game with our dad. It was hide-and-seek but with a twist. We called it "Hide, Seek, and Scare." As soon as the sun went down, we would turn off all the lights in the house and grab the flashlight. Someone was chosen to be "it." As the oldest sibling, I was always that person. With flashlight in hand, I'd count and everyone else would hide in dark closets and rooms. My job was to find everyone and scare them before they could jump out and scare me. So, as I crept through the house, I would find my brother and sisters, usually scaring them first. But my dad was a great hider, and he remained undiscovered every time. The four of us kids would scour the house, yelling for Dad, telling him we gave up and he could come out now. As the minutes of hunting passed, they started to feel like hours, and the tension mounted. Our fear grew more and more intense. Then all of a sudden, Dad would jump out of nowhere and tackle us into one big heap. We all screamed, scared half to death. After our shrieks subsided, the laughter began and we wrestled our big dad, having a great time.

I've realized that game of Hide, Seek, and Scare I played with my dad is similar to a game I play with God. Searching through the dark halls of life, I try to find God in all the places I am certain He must be. All the while I have that eerie feeling I'm being watched, so I act as if everything is okay and portray the cool, calm, and put-together person I think He wants to see. Yet I am scared of what will happen when I actually find God—or if He finds me. Is He going to jump out from behind the dark corner and tackle me? What will I feel when we find each other? Fear? Love? Acceptance? Inferiority?

C. S. Lewis once said,

> There comes a moment when the children who have been playing at burglars hush suddenly: was that a real footstep in the hall? There comes a moment when people who have been dabbling in religion ("Man's search for God!") suddenly draw back. Suppose that we really found Him? We never meant it to come to *that*! Worse still, supposing He found us?*

For many people, it's so much easier to pretend—pretend we're really looking for God, pretend we're something we're not with

* C. S. Lewis, *Miracles* (San Francisco: HarperOne, 2001), 150.

Him, pretend that keeping up a charade is just fine. But only when we find the true God, or allow Him to find us, will we have a chance to experience the fullness and abundance He promised.

THE JOY OF BEING FOUND

As raw as it may feel to be seen for who you really are, there is nothing more comforting than being accepted that way. A sense of peace, purpose, and joy come when we remove the images we manage and acknowledge that God already sees us the way we are behind our facades. Hebrews 4:13 says, "No creature is hidden from his sight, but all are naked and exposed to the eyes of him to whom we must give account." Because He is already aware of everything, we can rest assured our admissions and confessions do not surprise Him. Rather, it is by these very things that we experience true transformation in the areas we try to cover up the most.

By being honest we peel scales off our eyes that have distorted our view of God, and have therefore distorted our view of ourselves. We will have the proper motivation for our honesty if we regain the correct view of Who it is we're being honest with. If we will lay down our masks and truly seek God as He is, we will soon find God's cleansing (Psalm 51:10), the ability to pursue continued holiness (Jeremiah 6:16), and peaceful rest with the assurance that our guilt is removed by the blood of Christ (1 John 1:6–7).

I admit there have been many days even since the Columbine tragedy where I've merely upheld an image of godliness for others and for God to see. I tried to say all the right things and pray all the right ways because that's what I thought would keep me at peace with God. Another young believer was warned against this hundreds of years prior to me. Timothy received a letter from his mentor, the apostle Paul, telling him there will be people "having the appearance of godliness, but denying its power" (2 Timothy 3:5). Paul warned him to "avoid such people" and by implication avoid *being* such a person. While we may have momentary mismatches between our internal faith and external appearance, we must never make a habit of being something other than who we really are before both God and man.

The only way we will be able to do this is by humbly holding ourselves up to the light of who God is. While this will expose the holes and gaps that exist within us, it will allow those places to be filled with the transforming light of Christ to make us whole once again.

PART THREE

AN HONEST ENCOUNTER WITH GOD HIMSELF

CHAPTER 9

UNRAVELING THE MYSTERY OF AUTHENTICITY
WITH THE ALMIGHTY

It was bone-chilling cold outside, as most winter nights are in Chicago. I had just gotten off from waiting tables at a restaurant on Chicago's famous Magnificent Mile and was making the trek back to my apartment. I was disappointed that my tips were nothing more than a measly nineteen bucks. I just wanted to get home and have a cup of warm anything and call it a night.

With my head tucked down as low as I could get it into my scarf, I barely noticed the lady sitting on the sidewalk until I nearly stepped on her. The freezing temperature compelled my unfiltered response, "Ma'am, don't you have anywhere you can go to get out of the cold tonight? You could die out here."

She raised her head and looked at me. Her cheeks were as red as stoplights, with lips as chapped as someone who'd been skiing for a week straight. She replied, "No sir, I am homeless." Slightly embarrassed that I'd made her state the obvious, I was at a loss for words.

That, and I had no idea what to do for her. I paused for a moment with our eyes locked.

I knelt down to look in her eyes in hopes that a warm smile might be of help. "Is there anything I can do for you?" I feebly murmured.

She thought for a moment and then asked, "Are you wearing socks?"

"Socks? Um, yes," I said, looking down as if I had to check. "Yes, I am wearing socks. Why?"

"My toes are freezing. Can I have them, please?"

"Of course you can." I sat next to her and started untying my shoes. As people passed by (even a couple I had just served at the restaurant), they looked at me perplexed. An odd scene, for sure. I pulled off my socks, apologized if they smelled, and helped the woman put them on her icicle-like feet.

With parting words of encouragement, I bid the woman farewell. My feet were cold, but my heart was burning inside. I will never forget the walk home, because it was as if God had a few words with me. *Josh, you know I am good and gracious, but you don't live like you believe it because you complain about what you don't have rather than reveling in what I've given you. I am sovereign over the sun. I am sovereign over your socks as well.*

This was profound! You see, I was nothing more than a grumbling mess on my way home from work that night. Not only had I been whining about my lousy tips, but for weeks, maybe even months, my prayer life was full of nothing more than telling God all the areas in my life that weren't adding up. My schoolwork was insurmountable. My bills exceeded my income. The girl I wanted to marry wouldn't even date me. The loneliness I felt thousands of miles away from my family was killing me. Complaining had become a way of life—until I gave that lady my socks. Something happened when God reminded me that my finite problems were nothing compared to His infinite supremacy over the details of my life.

It doesn't matter that I've grown up in the church, attended Bible school, or preached hundreds of times about God. I still struggle to understand who He is and how that really affects me. Sure, I began believing in Him when I was a child, but as I've grown up there have been many things I've realized that I don't understand about Him. And when you have a God who is not easy to understand, if you are not intentional to pursue Him, He can seem very removed at times.

THE PERFECT STRANGER

Suppose you've just taken a seat at your favorite coffee shop one morning. There is a lot on your mind. Work has become a nightmare of conflict with the boss because your performance has been slipping. That's probably because things aren't going well in the rest of your life. Your relationship with your spouse has been under increasing stress for all the usual reasons—money, different goals, general fatigue, and creeping dissatisfaction. You're beginning to fear that your future is not as bright as you always expected it to be. A dark depression is threatening to overtake you.

In other words, you could really use some help.

Just then the door opens and in walks someone you vaguely recognize. You remember meeting him once, but can't come up with his name. You look away awkwardly, pretending not to have seen him, but to your amazement, he walks straight to your table and sits down beside you.

"Tell me all about it," he says, with no introduction.

"Excuse me?" You wonder if this is his idea of a practical joke.

"I'm here to listen," he says. "You can tell me anything at all. Trust me. What is on your mind?"

How would you most likely react?

a. quietly get up and move to another table

b. blurt out, "Pardon me, but do I know you?!"

c. say something like, "Dude, I don't *know* you. Why would I tell you anything?"

Granted, this imaginary scenario is unlikely to happen in real life. People generally don't behave like that; if they did we'd quickly put them at arm's length—and keep them there. Why? Because we have a hard enough time opening up and sharing our innermost thoughts and feelings with people we *know*—much less with strangers. The sort of trust that supports complete honesty grows slowly, like a well-tended garden. Between sowing the seed and reaping the fruit lies a lot of careful nurture and, above all, time.

Yet here is an important question to consider: Does something like the above scenario happen when you think about being completely open with God? Perhaps it sounds like a good idea and something you *should* do, but the same rules of trust and vulnerability apply to your relationship with Him as with other people. How well do you really know Him, after all? Well enough to be sure He can handle your high-voltage honesty? Do you believe that He really does care about your life and what you have to say, or do you just feel bad bothering Him? Does the thought of being transparent with Him make you want to rush into His arms—or to find somewhere else to sit in the hope that you can hang on to your anonymity a little longer?

The truth is, even if we do desire to be totally transparent with Him, there are many ways to misunderstand God's character and miss out on the benefits of an open, honest relationship with Him that is built on the truth of who He really is, not just what we expect Him to be. Too often we lower our view of God by looking at Him through what we've experienced with other human beings. The first step in seeing God for who He really is requires that you stop seeing Him as another version of us.

"IS GOD LIKE THAT?"

Claire stood patiently in line to speak with me after I preached at a youth rally. She let teen after teen go ahead of her until no one else remained except the workmen in the school gym putting away chairs and sweeping the floor. The clatter of cleanup echoed around us when her turn finally arrived. She was around sixteen, dressed in Goth black from head to toe, eyes blazing through heavy black make-up. Her piercing look let me know she was not happy with something I said. I had just given a sermon on the love of God and an invitation to experience His love by being completely open with Him.

I tried to start with a simple, "Hey, how are you?" but she didn't even go for the small talk. "I can't be honest with God," she said flatly. "I can't even love Him, not the way you talk about."

She seemed fiercely determined to defend her position, but behind her sharp words and the tears that were building in her eyes, I could hear the part she'd left unspoken: "I can't love God . . . *but I want to!*"

"Really?" I asked. "Why not?"

"You keep calling Him our 'Father,'" she said, contempt dripping from the word. "When I was a kid my father said he loved me and bought me stuff all the time, but he was never home. When he was there he yelled and even hit my mom at night when they thought I couldn't hear, and the next morning he would pretend nothing was wrong. Then one day he left us for another woman. I still get letters once in a while telling me he loves me.

"Is *God* like that?" she asked. "Does He only *say* He loves me, without really meaning it?"

"No, God is nothing like that," I replied softly.

"My boyfriend is a nice guy," she continued. "He treats me well and says he loves me. He said he would never do anything to hurt me. But we were in his car last weekend and he started to take advantage of me. I told him to stop and I didn't want to, but he said if I really loved him, I'd let him have sex with me. Is God like that? Does He just say He loves me to get what He wants from me?"

"No, that's not who God is either."

She was now weeping, and her emotion caused me to well up with tears. She stood there and cried for a minute. I thought the story was over, but finally when she mustered up the ability to talk through her tears, she kept going.

"What about the youth pastor at my church?" she challenged, voice rising in pitch as she grew more and more desperate for answers. "I went to him to tell him about my dad and my boyfriend. I shared with him some of my deepest thoughts . . . and even my desire to stop living. There in the church office, he told me I was loved by God and by him. He got all close and started hugging me and kissing my forehead. Before I knew it he was kissing my mouth. I was so freaked out! I was so mad!"

Then she crescendoed in anger and desperation, "Is God like *that*?"

With tears now rolling down my cheeks, I said, "God is nothing like that." I spent the next half hour opening God's Word for her and showing her verse after verse in the Bible about God's perfection. I led her to the deep end of God's love and invited her to dive in. She left there that night with an understanding that God is nothing like the warped humans of this world. He is "Wholly Other." I connected her with the proper pastoral staff who would help her continue to grow in the knowledge of God and ensure that the youth pastor and others were rightly removed from her life.

Later on as I reflected on that night, I realized that girl was only saying out loud what many people struggle with in silence: an inability to be open with *anyone*—God included—because of how many times their earthly attempts at love and trust have ended in betrayal. Claire's story is an extreme example of how God is frequently mistaken for someone else. This assumption doesn't change the character of God; rather, it steals from us the ability to feel safe, and be honest, in relationship with Him.

WHO GOD REALLY IS—AND ISN'T

So, before taking another step toward getting real with God, let's be sure we see Him clearly—beginning with a picture of what He *never* is. He is never:

Abusive
Untruthful
Manipulative
Cruel
Greedy
Controlling
Nasty
Spiteful
Wicked

The list could go on and on. Pick a negative personality trait you've encountered and fill in the blank: God is not _____. Of course, there is a simple shortcut that covers every possibility at once: God is not *like us*. That says it all. Though we are made in His image, sin is a part of who we are. But sin has never been a part of who He is—ever. He is perpetually perfect. But understanding what God is *not* only gets us halfway home.

While there is no way that I can give an exhaustive treatment to God's attributes here, allow me to point out a few things we must know about Him if we are going to be honest with Him for the sake of change. Here's a list of what He *is*:

Holy. Of all our Creator's attributes, this is perhaps the hardest to understand—and the one most likely to frighten us into hiding in the shadows, as Adam and Eve did. We read in the Bible that He is "holy," inspiring even the angels to fall on their faces in His presence, but that's not exactly the most inviting image when you've got troubling and secret things to say to Him. But thanks to the new covenant Jesus established by His death and resurrection, God's holiness is no longer an impassable barrier. Now, because of Christ's sacrifice covering our sin, He sees *us* as holy too, no matter how unworthy we think we are. *His holiness is important for my honesty because I can be assured my filth is no longer seen because I am covered by Christ's righteousness.*

Sovereign. Nothing surprises God or threatens Him. Nothing ever spins out of His control or ruins His plan to restore all things and establish His kingdom on earth—just as it is in heaven. Nothing depletes Him or wounds Him. Nothing is ever beyond His ability to work out for our good. This is not to say that God causes all things to happen. The Bible is clear that God does not cause us to lie or steal, or do any other sinful thing. However, it does say that even the very worst possible thing that occurs, God is able to transform for our good. *Therefore, His sovereignty is important for my honesty because it allows me to share anything with Him and trust He is watching over the process and the outcome.*

Present. God is never distracted or preoccupied, never too busy for me, never "here one minute and gone the next." He is deeply interested in my life down to the tiniest detail. He never leaves us or forsakes us. *His attentiveness is important for my honesty because it gives me the freedom to share anything at any time.*

Giving and Forgiving. God's eternal grace and daily blessings can never be thwarted or exhausted. There are no strings attached to His gifts or His forgiveness. He holds no grudges. Like the father in the parable of the prodigal son, He runs to us and lavishes His love on us when we sincerely seek Him. *His forgiveness is important for my honesty because it removes the roadblock of my shame and allows me to find freedom from my faults.*

Love. This is the most important point of all, without which your picture of who God is will always be incomplete. He is not simply *loving*. That can be said of people too, from time to time. That kind of love is something we do—or don't do—depending on how we feel at the time. But God *is* Love. It is the very fabric of His being.

This is an essential point for us in our quest to feel safe enough to be completely honest with God: It is *impossible* for Him to be unloving, not even for the briefest moment of time or in the smallest possible measurement. Even when He disciplines His followers or destroys nations, He does it all without compromising His love. All of His attributes work together in harmony. His love isn't dependent on whim or feelings. It is who He is. *That* is what sets Him apart from people. *His love allows me to be completely honest because I can trust Him unconditionally where others have failed me.*

Knowing God is a lifelong pursuit. Still, this side of heaven, we will only ever see Him imperfectly, "in a mirror dimly," as the apostle Paul aptly said (1 Corinthians 13:12). But one thing is certain: Open and honest conversation with Him—unhindered by fear and unclouded by doubt or misconception—is an excellent place to start. As we have noted often, honesty is not simply an end in itself; it is a marvelous step on the pathway back to the kind of fellowship we enjoyed with our Father in Eden. He reveals Himself to us in the midst of our struggles (Psalm 46:1). He is faithful to give new insights into His character to those who question Him (Job 42:2–3, 5), wrestle with Him (Genesis 32:22–32).

Only you have the power to lower your defenses and reveal your true self to God. Allow this big God to prove Himself to you in the big and little things of your life. It is time to start being honest to God by aligning your perspective to who He really is. If you do, you'll never be the same.

CHAPTER 10

TOO CLOSE FOR COMFORT?

GOD KNOWS ME BETTER THAN I KNOW MYSELF

Everything about the man's aura and appearance said *Professor*. It also said *wise*, *insightful*, and *dignified*.

I had been on staff with Dr. W. Bingham Hunter at Harvest Bible Chapel in Rolling Meadows, Illinois, for a year, and I had admired and respected him from a distance. After all, here was a man who had written beloved books, served as dean at top seminaries, and wrote theological papers for scholarly journals. Tall and lanky, with graying red hair and a bushy mustache, often attired in a sweater vest or sports coat with a tie, the only thing missing to complete the academic ensemble was a pipe.

Because we had different areas of ministry responsibility, I'd rarely interacted with Dr. Hunter (I could never quite bring myself to call him "Bing," as he preferred). However, around that time I had begun thinking deeply about the topic of being totally open with God and had even started a radio program called *Honest to God*, so I saw an opportunity to glean wisdom from this gentle giant of a man. Following an all-staff meeting, I approached Dr. Hunter and asked if we could get together sometime.

"I'd be delighted," he said immediately. "Let's compare calendars." Flipping pages, he spotted an opening in his crowded schedule and penciled me in.

A week later, I was in his office, which was filled wall to wall, floor to ceiling, with books. We talked for less than an hour, and he offered words about what it means to speak with God like a trusting child to a loving father, the things that hold us back from total openness, and the freedom we have to approach the Lord with everything on our heart. I was thrilled—this respected thinker confirmed much of what I'd been concluding on the subject.

But of all the things Dr. Hunter said that day, one is forever burned into my memory. As I stood to leave his office, he came to stand beside me. With a twinkle in his eyes, he said with a winsome chuckle, "Josh, what can you tell a God who knows everything?" He paused for effect and then answered his own question: "You can tell him anything—*aaaaaanything*—because He knows everything! He knows everything about you already!"

Tell Him anything.

Because He knows everything.

That's the very essence of what *honest to God* means.

I'VE GOT YOU UNDER MY SKIN

I have recalled that moment with Dr. Hunter many times. And I've shared that thought with lots of people. For some, it's a source of great comfort realizing that God already knows everything there is to know about us. For others, it's a source of anxiety and apprehension. I'm pretty sure I know what these people are thinking: "There are some things I don't *want* God to know! Can't I have some privacy, at least in a few areas? What if God doesn't like what He sees?" There are still others—like myself—who carry some kind of guilt over the fact that God has to know everything about them. We feel we are too much of a burden for God. We view ourselves as nothing more than a peon taking God away from more important things in the world.

Those are understandable questions and concerns. Most of us, after all, have felt the sting of not being completely accepted, not feeling *acceptable*. We've had friends or even family members walk away from us because we couldn't be whom they wanted us to be or get it together quick enough for them. That hurts.

One of the greatest enemies of honesty is fear, and one of the greatest fears we battle is the fear of rejection.

What if people knew what we really did in a day?

Or what we were thinking while riding the bus?

Or what we felt when we walk through the front door?

Would they reject us because they would be shocked, or maybe bored? Would they think badly of us or, even worse, would they stop thinking of us altogether? Abandon and ignore us?

The fear of rejection is one of the most common fears, and it seems that few people are immune from it. Actress Reese Witherspoon says that "the most horrifying thing" ever said to her was shortly after her divorce. Someone told her, "Oh, no man will ever accept your children." In her case, though, Witherspoon says her fear made her determined to "find somebody who would make that not true. And I got lucky. I did. I got very lucky, and he's wonderful. And so wonderful with the children. I'm very blessed."

Apparently, Witherspoon didn't let her fear get in the way of pursuing intimacy. But for many of us the fear of rejection doesn't drive us *toward* intimacy, but away. It doesn't propel us toward vulnerability, but toward facades. We scramble to please, to pretend we're really okay, while the real us is in hiding. We build walls to protect and to pretend, but even a beautiful wall is a barrier to honesty.

Another actress, Kristen Scott Thomas, chosen by *People* magazine as one of the 50 Most Beautiful People in the world, admits she was so afraid of rejection that she used to avoid calling people to suggest getting together because she was afraid they'd make up an excuse not to. She couldn't bear the rejection. She says that, to deal with her fear, she "created a haze" around herself and "didn't acknowledge people." The image she projected was one of being aloof. But that was an illusion. In reality, she was afraid.

I've done the same thing. Afraid of being pushed away, I distanced myself. Afraid of being judged, I hid parts of me. Afraid of being forgotten, I presented myself as someone I am not. Justified or not, the fear of rejection is powerful and can keep us isolated. Disconnected. Disguised. Dishonest.

But what if that fear could be alleviated? What if you knew there was someone who already knew everything about you and—here's the key—hadn't rejected you? And not only didn't reject you, but embraced you. Imagine that!

Someone who knew what you *really* did in a day?

And what you were thinking?

And what you felt?

And what you did in your free time?

What if this person knew everything and still had nothing but consistently loving thoughts about you? What if the possibility of rejection were no longer an issue, and abandonment simply wasn't a possibility?

Too good to be true?

As I've pointed out previously, King David of the Old Testament is known for his gut-wrenchingly honest conversations with God. In poems, prayers, and songs, he pours out his heart, time and again, to his God. Sometimes he's angry, sometimes jubilant, sometimes discouraged. But he's never less than honest.

What's his secret? What drives this level of transparency and authenticity?

If you ask me, David's secret is found in Psalm 139. In these twenty-four verses, David describes a God who knows him intimately and loves him anyway. He describes One who never turns His back, who invites us instead with open arms ready to hold us tight. He describes an all-knowing, omnipresent Father who simply can't be shocked by anything we tell Him.

What does David know about God that you and I need to know? Let me highlight four things:

GOD SEARCHES AND UNDERSTANDS US

David gives a beautiful description of just how much God really cares and knows (see vv. 1–4). God knows what David does with his time, what he thinks, where he's going, when he rests, and everything he says or even is about to say. This is not a picture of an uninterested God who happens to observe what we're doing, with little care or interest. Quite the opposite. David paints a picture of a Creator who knows these things about us because He has made the effort to be aware of these details of our lives.

GOD IS EVERYWHERE

In verses 5 through 12, David writes about God's omnipresence. What David seems to be saying here is that, even if he *wanted* to do something (think something, go somewhere, or speak a word without God knowing), well, it's not going to happen. That's because God is everywhere we are and knows everything about who we are. That's not a matter of Big Brother hovering over us, scrutinizing us so He can play "gotcha" when we blow it. No, He tenderly holds our hand through all the ups and downs of this journey we're on.

David asks, "Where shall I go from your Spirit? Or where shall I flee from your presence? If I ascend to heaven, you are there! If I make my bed in Sheol, you are there!" Even if we wanted to get away from His presence, we couldn't. But there's no need to run and hide; He's with us always, and always with grace and compassion.

GOD CREATED US IN OUR MOTHER'S WOMB

There's much more. God put a lot of loving thought into the process of creating us to be the unique individuals we are. As David puts it, "I am fearfully and wonderfully made. Wonderful are your works." He adds, "My frame was not hidden from you, when I was being made in secret, intricately woven in the depths of the earth (vv. 14–15)."

I get this sentiment, at least partially. I've had the awesome privilege of looking at the sonograms for each of my two children. Both times, I've been transfixed by the grainy, black-and-white printout that showed my child—my own child—growing and forming in my wife's womb. It's almost too much to wrap my head around. That's a tiny, amazing, beautiful little person in there, and I had a part in the creation process. I felt so overwhelmed, I cried. It was embarrassing to ask for a tissue each time, but I didn't care; I was witnessing God's handiwork firsthand.

I imagine that's the kind of joy God feels too. Our Creator, the One who gives life to each of us, was ecstatic to see us take shape in our mother's womb. Every face you see on the street is one designed by God. Our noses, jawlines, and earlobes are all handcrafted by God in that secret, hidden place. He continues to be elated as we grow, develop, and mature throughout our lives.

God fashioned not only our bodies but our destinies as well. "Your eyes saw my unformed substance; in your book were written, every one of them, the days that were formed for me, when as yet there was none of them (v. 16)." He knows the whole scope of our lives—the good, the bad, and the ugly—and still loves us in spite of our actions. He's still overjoyed about who we are, just as He was when we hadn't yet done anything wrong, when we were still innocently and safely basking in our mother's womb.

David certainly drives the point home: God knows us even better than we know ourselves.

Now what?

Is this where the rejection takes place? After all, with God knowing us this well, doesn't it increase the chances that He'll abandon us, that He'll eventually erase us from His thoughts? No. In fact, quite the opposite is true.

HE HOLDS, GUIDES, AND PROTECTS

Throughout this psalm, David affirms that God's response to knowing us thoroughly is to love us just as thoroughly. In fact, David gives us a beautiful image of God's protective nature, describing God not only enfolding us from the front and back, but also putting His hand on our head (v. 5). He says God's hand leads us and holds us (v. 10). We are given this reassurance: "How precious to me are your thoughts, O God! How vast is the sum of them! If I would count them, they are more than the sand. I awake, and I am still with you" (vv. 17–18).

Surprisingly, God's response to knowing you as well as He does is to remain close. What is David's response to being known and loved in such a beautiful manner? Complete openness. He goes on to speak with heart-wrenching honesty about troubles he's had with bloodthirsty men who hate God. Then he admits he has anxieties (v. 23). Finally, he invites God to search him, know his heart, and continue leading him forward (vv. 23–24).

What is your response to the God who knows everything about

you and loves you anyway? Since God knows everything about you, and still loves you, are you free to tell Him anything and everything, without fear or limitations? Are you ready to tell Him about your anxieties? Invite Him to search your heart? Celebrate His many precious thoughts toward you?

As you ponder those questions, chew on something else Dr. Hunter has said: "Prayer is communication from a whole person to the Wholeness which is the living God."* We can bring our whole selves to our Father—our hurts, frustrations, disappointments, failures—because He knows us completely and loves us intimately.

We can rest assured that we are not throwaways to God. He spent His Son to pay to justify us, and to count us as righteous, holy, and pure. He views us as valuable and costly, not simply something to toss aside as a minor annoyance. God does not reject us and never will.

* W. Bingham Hunter, *The God Who Hears* (Downers Grove, IL: InterVarsity, 1986), back cover.

CHAPTER 11

THE SCANDAL OF GRACE

THE KEY OF GOD'S FORGIVENESS
WILL UNLOCK YOUR HONEST HEART

Grace can seem a lot like a mirage dancing on the desert horizon. Like cool water, it shimmers, promising refreshing relief to all who are thirsty. Yet the full meaning of God's grace is often mysterious and elusive. In hundreds of sermons and books we've heard that God's grace is *free, and unconditional, a gift not to be bought or earned*, but still, we don't quite believe it. It can't possibly be as simple as it sounds, we think. There must be a catch—there's *always* a catch!

Nope. Not this time.

In actuality, grace isn't a mirage at all; it is an oasis. However, grace cannot be found through cleverness or hard work or any amount of "goodness." The pathway opens only when you drop your lifelong burdens of guilt, fear, and shame—and your misplaced hope in self-righteousness—and let Christ lead the way. I can hear your objections now:

"I've heard it before, but I still don't totally grasp how God's grace is big enough to cover my mess. Do you really believe there is nothing I must say or do or be in order to receive God's grace? And nothing I can do in the future to cause Him to take it back?"

Yes, I do. *Nothing*.

"So if that is true, won't people take advantage of a loophole like that and just go right on sinning?"

Ah, now you've discovered why I describe grace as "scandalous."

"NOT APPROPRIATE FOR DISSEMINATION"

I was sitting at a small coffee shop in Castle Rock, Colorado, with my friend Alan as we discussed the idea of grace. He has certainly seen the hand of God supply provision for his messes a time or two. I identified with the way he's seen grace so vividly by telling him a few stories of my own. As we both sat there, moved by God's free gift of grace, I blurted out in frustration, "But it can be so hard as a preacher—or even a Christian—to communicate this unmerited grace to a world that's used to having to work for something." With that, Alan lit up and said, "Let me tell you how one church I went to handled the idea of this scandalous grace."

A guest minister was speaking one Sunday at our church. He began his sermon with one statement: "Upon hearing about grace, if your mind doesn't accuse you of trying to get away with something, then you haven't properly understood it yet." He repeated the sentence several times until you could have heard a pin drop in the auditorium. Each time he said it, his pace was slower and his tone more emphatic: "Upon hearing about grace, if your mind doesn't accuse you of trying to get away with something, then you haven't properly understood it yet."

Over the next half hour he explained this haunting statement, convinced me that grace was far more encompassing than I knew, and because of that fact, God was far more approachable than I had believed. I had nothing to fear from my past sin, or even from my future ones! Ever.

I was thrilled! It opened up my relationship with God in ways that had eluded me until then. In order to share the message with my wife—who had been working in the nursery during the service that morning—the next Sunday I went to the table in the lobby where recordings of previous sermons were available. When I asked for the recording from last week, the woman looked embarrassed and said, "Oh, the church leaders decided that message was not appropriate for dissemination."

I could hardly believe my ears, but I understood then why the minister had titled his sermon, "The *Scandal* of Grace."

Clearly, even church leaders are prone to placing limits on the magnitude of God's grace, and they fear what might happen if people suddenly took it to be a license to live as they please. Even some of the earliest Christians had to be rebuked by the apostle Paul for seeing grace as a permission slip to keep on sinning (Romans 6:1).

God's grace is not a loophole to allow us more of what we want without consequence. Rather, grace is the kindness of the Lord that should bring us to the place of surrender. When we've been forgiven by our loving Father for the wrong we've done, we should want nothing more than to never do wrong again because of the forgiveness we've been shown. Grace should propel us toward God, not away from Him.

In the same way, we obviously don't understand His mercy and grace when we run scared that God is going to backhand us for our sin. This happens when, after committing an offense against God, we dwell on thoughts of judgment and punishment rather than the cross of Christ. It is our small view of God that keeps us from seeing Him as the merciful Redeemer that He truly is. This inadequate idea of grace will keep us superificial with the Almighty because we live in fear of Him striking us with judgment whenever we fall short.

In effect, we rebuild the prison walls of guilt and fear that Jesus came to tear down. By doing this, we exalt our works and see Christ's grace as nothing more than a scandal, getting away with something we shouldn't. But that is exactly it! We don't deserve it. Neither did the many people whom Jesus healed in the Gospels, but that is exactly why the Jewish leaders of that time thought Jesus was a fake! They thought that because He didn't preach the righteousness by good works that they did, that He was surely deceiving people.

Here's the bottom line: *Grasping the totality of God's grace is an essential step in learning to be honest with Him.* So long as I fear His disapproval, I will never have the courage to tell Him exactly what's on my mind.

But as I've already implied, one more sermon or one more clever theological argument is unlikely to finally tip the balance toward real understanding. Instead, allow me to try a different approach—a story, in which the main character is *you*.

THE CANYON'S EDGE

Imagine you're walking alone on a dry and rocky dirt road rising upward across a barren, windswept hillside. Overhead, the sun pounds you with punishing heat. Ruts cut deep into the parched road, making each step a miserable struggle. What's worse, you are dragging a giant burlap bag, rattling and clanking and thumping along behind you. It is filled with damaged and useless junk: dented pots and pans, a half dozen bald tires, ragged clothes that are torn and don't fit you anyway, faded photographs of people you once knew now staring blankly through broken glass frames, and numerous old suitcases stuffed with who knows what. The bag scrapes along in a rut as you walk. Why does the hill never seem to end? Why does the bag keep filling with more and more stuff, growing heavier by the hour?

You are on the verge of weeping with weariness.

Then, ahead of you on the road, you see a man. He carries no bag and walks toward you out of the blinding sun. Even from a distance, you can see there is something strange and different about him. His movements are effortless and as light as air. His face shows no sign of misery or fatigue, but seems to glow from within. And his eyes are fixed upon *you*. In an instant, he is at your side.

"Are you tired of carrying that yet?" he asks with a smile that bubbles up like a cold spring out of the rocky ground. He tenderly speaks your name and holds out his hand.

You raise your arm to wipe sweat from your eyes, and realize instead it is a torrent of tears running down your face. "Yes!" you cry, desperate for relief.

"Then I'll take over for a while." He lifts the bag onto his shoulders as if it were filled with soap bubbles. He sets out again in the direction you were headed.

"Well, come on then," he says, looking back at you.

"Where are we going?" you ask.

"You'll see."

For a while you walk and talk together. You are grateful not to be dragging the bag like an anchor through the desert, and for the company after being alone on the road so long. The man wants to hear all about you, and the conversation melts away the miles. Then he stops.

"We're here," he says.

You turn and see you've arrived at the edge of a massive canyon, deeper and wider than anything you've ever imagined. It has no bottom that you can see. The emptiness reminds you of stories you've heard about black holes in space from which even light can't escape. What goes in never returns—ever.

The man sets the bag down beside you. You move to pick it up again, and it is heavier than ever.

"You've dragged that stuff around long enough, don't you think? That's not what God wants for you. How about letting it go?"

You realize that, in spite of all the times you've cursed the bag and everything in it, you feel strangely attached to what's inside. It's not that you *like* it, but it is *yours*. You made every bit of it yourself, and you deserve to drag it around for as long as you live. It wouldn't be right for someone else to carry it for you.

As if reading your mind, the man says, "I'm not talking about carrying it for you. Your God has made a way for it to *disappear*. Forever. Are you interested?"

You hesitate. He reaches into the bag and pulls out something that resembles a bicycle that's been run over by a dump truck—more than once, by the look of it. "What's this thing?" he asks.

"That's the time I stole a hundred dollars from my grandmother's purse," you reply, feeling a deep and familiar shame. "She knew, but never said a word to me or my parents. She kept right on loving me and praying for me like nothing had happened."

"Hmm," he says, with an approving nod. "And this?"

He takes out a battered metal box, wrapped in padlocked chains. You quickly take it from him. What's locked inside is a secret no one must ever see. *No one.*

"It's okay," he says gently. "God has already seen it. Would you like to be rid of it forever?"

"But how?" you ask. "It's not like this other stuff. It's really *bad*."

The man smiles, and you feel lighter on your feet, like a cool wind suddenly swirling around you on a hot day.

"Yes it is," he says, his eyes never leaving yours. "So what? Just throw it in the canyon."

"What if it was a stupid decision that really hurt someone?"

"Toss it."

"What if it's my secret addiction to pornography?"

"Bombs away!"

"What if it was even something like adultery or murder?!"

"What are you waiting for?"

"So you're saying it could be anything at all?"

"Is what you have in there larger than God's love? I don't think so. Let it go!"

At first the invitation feels entirely too uncomfortable. You consider running, but you are sure you'll only look foolish as you try to jog away with all your junk. He waits while you contemplate his invitation. You feel tears begin to well up as you realize the mess you've made with no apparent way out except the one he is offering you.

But you also detect a tingling sensation arising in the middle of your chest. It grows and spreads through your whole body as you begin to grasp the magnitude of this news. No more bag? No more dragging this miserable load? No more fear or reason to hide from God? You burst into laughter, and Jesus is laughing too. The laughter is billowing up from the deepest part of you as you are overcome with the joy of being found out and let out. The laughter and the tears flow as you understand the immensity of His grace. In comparison, your bag seems much smaller now. He holds the bag open for you as you retrieve burden after burden and heave them out into the bottomless canyon of God's forgiveness—never to be seen or heard from again.

At last, the bag lies empty at your feet. You feel light enough to spread your arms and fly. But then a shadow of doubt starts to creep across your mind. You've been walking this road long enough to know the bag won't stay empty for long. Sooner or later you'll make another mistake, and another, and you'll be right back where you started.

Jesus laughs and throws His arm around your shoulder, once

more knowing what you're thinking. "Don't be afraid," He says. "From this day forward, all the useless junk that used to go into the bag will go straight into this canyon. In fact, it was there all along— you just didn't realize it."

"Things I haven't even done yet?"

"All of it. Forever."

"That doesn't seem right," you say, remembering the cynical words you've heard your whole life: "If it sounds too good to be true, it is."

"Of course it doesn't," Jesus replies with a smile. "If it did, it wouldn't be *grace*, now would it?"

DIVING INTO GRACE

Baring all before God means that you are going to unearth some messy stuff. Yes, there will be times you pray things you never wanted to hear yourself say. But here is something we can be assured of: God is never going to tell you to go away, clean up your act, and come back when you're ready. Never.

David knew the depth of the canyon of God's love and forgiveness when he wrote: "For as high as the heavens are above the earth, so great is his steadfast love toward those who fear him; as far as the east is from the west, so far does he remove our transgressions from us" (Psalm 103:11–12).

And Paul understood as well: "If we are faithless, he remains faithful" (2 Timothy 2:13). That's because He can't stop being the gracious God He is and always will be. This doesn't make me want to go on sinning—just the opposite! I want nothing more than to dive into that grace and remain faithful, whatever it costs.

We must preach this good news to ourselves daily because our sin *does* come back. Every day we must reclaim the power of Christ's life and death over the things that bring us shame. God's grace is a day-in-day-out acceptance, a moment-by-moment choosing to trust, choosing to believe. Continually I must remember that I am accepted whether I do all the right things or not; even on my best day, the very best decisions I make do not in any way determine my ultimate worth. I am sustained by Love Himself. Our greatest joy comes not from the freedom, or the relief of our burden, but by this Person who meets us on the road when we are dirty, tired, and burdened. It is His grace that invites us to live honest lives before God.

Our past is buried with Him and our future is resurrected in Him. By believing in Jesus and leaving our sin behind, we become one with Christ and have the same power He had over death to conquer our sin, guilt, and shame. Because we are loved by an all-knowing God, everything can be relinquished into His grace.

God's scandalous grace is the proof we need that we are *safe* with Him—enough to be honest about anything, anytime.

PART FOUR

BARING YOUR SOUL
FOR THE SAKE OF CHANGE

CHAPTER 12

GOD'S HONESTY PLAN

YOUR YELLOW BRICK ROAD TO FREEDOM

Everyone knows what a straightjacket is: a device commonly used to restrain mentally ill people who otherwise might harm themselves or others. Thanks to countless scenes on television and in movies, the word "straightjacket" usually conjures up mental pictures of crazed and wild-eyed characters babbling nonsense—or maybe an ice-cold serial killer who is let out of solitary confinement long enough to advise a nervous FBI agent on the workings of a deranged mind.

But I'm guessing you'd never in a million years visualize a preacher onstage in front of hundreds of people, sharing the gospel of Christ while wearing a straightjacket. And yet, I assure you, it has happened. The straightjacket was quite real, and the preacher was me.

I know firsthand how unsettling it is to slip my arms into the stiff canvas sleeves and allow someone to tighten the heavy leather straps across my back (in front of thousands of people, no less). I've experienced the instinctive panic when my hands are pulled roughly to my sides in an involuntary hug from which I might not escape. And I have seen the nervous fascination on faces in the crowd when I've walked onstage—nearly one hundred times now—immobilized in a real-life straightjacket.

Am I just an imitation Houdini, mixing macabre entertainment with ministry? Hardly. My purpose is simple—to visually reinforce a vitally important message: *sin is a straightjacket on your life.*

Sin and its attending separation from God binds and limits us in ways we can barely begin to fathom. It stifles our potential and saps our spiritual strength. It locks us into self-destructive behavior and the negative consequences that inevitably follow. No one is immune. No one is a special case—not even an unorthodox preacher!

But to say that "sin is a straightjacket" is only half the message. Many Christians stop there and spend years contemplating the *problem* in excruciating detail. They are usually the gloomy ones in the bunch who are so focused on their own unworthiness as sinners that they've forgotten the second half of the message, the joyful half containing immeasurably good news:

Sin is a straightjacket on your life, but God has a plan to set you free, *forever!*

FREE AT LAST

Honesty with God is not an end in itself. It isn't just a special kind of prayer or meditation. God's honesty plan is about much more than improved communication or transparency; it's about nothing less than the full spectrum of *transforming* your life. Honesty is the means by which you move out of hiding and become free to enter into deeper communion with your Creator than you ever thought possible.

But honesty isn't a once-and-for-all event. It is a way of life, a series of choices you must make again and again with each new challenge that you face. The following is a list of practical steps that have the potential to lead you away from your present life of bondage and into a deeper intimacy with God, with nothing left to stand between you and the abundant life Jesus made possible by His death and resurrection.

Each of these stages will make you feel uncomfortably vulnerable and exposed, but will also bring you that much closer to the beneficial goal: deep and lasting connection with God. Before I unveil these things, let me tell you that I was hesitant to reduce these to steps, because a relationship with God can never be reduced to a checklist religion. However, when you are trapped, the best way to get out is to follow a plan—God's plan—to find true freedom. But the only way the following items will actually work is if you actually take them to heart. These are not steps to simply *do*; the following are ways we must *be* before God so that we may have a deep relationship with Him. Take your time with each step; this is not an instant pudding kind of faith. Allow God to truly reveal to you the things about Himself and yourself that need to be exposed. Shall we begin?

1. *Admit you're hiding.* Many Christians spend years without ever attempting a more open and honest relationship with God because they aren't even aware of the layers of cover and concealment they've been living under. They've hidden so long it has become their "normal" state of being; they don't even realize something far better *is possible*. This isn't surprising. The human heart, which Jeremiah 17:9 tells us is "deceitful above all things," knows all the best hiding places and has many disguises with which to camouflage the truth.

Some people prefer a mask of guilt and shame. They know better than anyone they are naked and sinful, and never let themselves forget it. Others put on a cloak of conspicuous spirituality, hoping to keep God at arm's length by pretending their relationship with Him is already fully open and thriving. Some hide behind nonstop work, others in caves of introversion and isolation. The truth is, there are as many ways to avoid authenticity with God as there are people.

The necessary first step in being honest with God is to look in the mirror and realize you are wearing a mask. Are you being as authentic with God as you'd like to be? You need to realize that God views the face behind the mask as more beautiful than the mask you're wearing.

2. *Answer God when He calls.* As we saw in chapter 2, perhaps the most astonishing detail in the story of Adam and Eve eating the fruit of the forbidden tree was not that they ran and hid from God once they realized their mistake. It was that God came looking for them anyway. He lovingly sought them out in spite of their sin, foreshadowing, even then, the day when He would send His Son to rescue the human race. God called their names in the garden, as He calls to each of us to this day.

Here's the part your choice plays in the process: You don't *have to* answer. God will never barge into your hiding place and drag you out. You can shrink into the bushes and keep quiet, wherever you are, for the rest of your life if you so desire. But that way of living gets old, doesn't it? Aren't you tired of feeling isolated and alone? Don't you long for the deep intimacy with God you thought would come automatically when you first believed? Here is the next step that will bring you that much closer to your wish: simply say, "Here I am."

3. *Acknowledge your sin.* Back in Eden, when God found His ashamed and terrified children, He asked them, "Have you eaten of the tree of which I commanded you not to eat?" Of course the Creator already knew the answer. But then and now, humble confession and repentance are key components of our reconciliation with God.

A brazen kind of honesty with God that says, "Yeah, I sinned. So what?" is not a path to freedom at all. As painful as it can be, we must always be willing to tell the truth and own up to our sinful activity.

"Did you do the things I told you not to do?" Yes, we all have. Yet these are not the words of an angry, vindictive God but of a loving Father who wants to get the healing conversation started. Why? So we can move past our guilt and into redemption!

Confessing your sinfulness to God is never easy. But it is a key step on the road to freedom—the road that leads to intimacy with our Redeemer.

4. *Accept the gift of grace.* As I've already suggested, admitting your sin and recognizing your need are necessary steps, but they are by no means the end of the line. In fact, they simply set the stage for the most important part of God's plan to break open your cage: His radical and unconditional forgiveness, available to anyone willing to believe. Yes, this means *you*. Yet, just because someone offers you a precious gift, doesn't mean you have to take it.

It is sad to see the number of Christians who resist truly trusting God's grace, feeling it can't possibly apply to *them*, only to people who are more deserving. But appropriating the grace of God is not a passive act. It requires a deliberate and ongoing choice to keep God's grace fresh in your mind. You must purposely decide to embrace the reality that your sins are *gone*, and then live accordingly.

5. *Abandon your defenses.* The final step on the road to freedom and transformation through honesty with God is the culmination of all the others. This is the moment of action when you get up and leave your hiding place behind. It is simultaneously a time of maximum vulnerability and utmost intimacy with God. Honesty has led you home again—naked and unashamed—to the garden of communion with Him. No longer do you pray what is safe but are willing to tell God how you honestly feel. As intrusive as it may seem, when you abandon your defenses, you will enjoy inviting the Holy Spirit to be involved in the deep things within you so that you may know the deeps things of God (1 Corinthians 2:10–12).

Repeat these steps as often as necessary; repetition does not mean failure, but is essential for continual consecration to God. We are a forgetful people. We have seasons of openness with God, but our sinful actions and sealed-off attitudes have a way of creeping back in. Expect the cycle to be repeated and be freer in it and deeper through it each time. Do not dread beginning again. Admit you've hidden and return to God more passionately than the last time.

Once you've tasted the fruit of surrender and transparency before your Creator, your heart will cry out like David's, "A day in your courts is better than a thousand elsewhere. I would rather be a door-keeper in the house of my God than dwell in the tents of wickedness" (Psalm 84:10). In other words, by coming out into the open before God, you'll be *transformed*, preferring unreserved relationship with Him to every other thing.

A FRUITFUL PLAN

Who would *want* to wear a straightjacket through life when the straps have been released? Who *likes* carrying a constant and heavy burden of sin and shame? I'm guessing the answer is, *No one*! We all long to enter God's presence freely and fully—that's why we became believers in the first place.

Here's the good news: God's honesty plan is how we get there. Paul wrote, "For freedom Christ has set us free; stand firm therefore, and do not submit again to a yoke of slavery" (Galatians 5:1). Honesty with God is one way we "stand firm." Choosing to accept the risk of vulnerability and baring ourselves before Him is the active role we play in keeping off the yoke of slavery to guilt and shame.

One day at a time, one step at a time, follow God's plan into the precious freedom Christ bought for you and reclaim it daily. His mercies are new every morning.

CHAPTER 13

THE **PROCESS** OF **PURGING**

REMOVING THE JUNK FROM YOUR INNER SPACE ALLOWS GOD TO REMODEL

"Don't forget, Saturday is purge day."

I said that to my wife a few weeks ago, referring to a big challenge we'd set for ourselves. We were ready to address something we had been avoiding for quite some time.

But first I better clarify. These days if you use the word *purge*, you need to put it in context. That's because some people might link it with another word in popular usage, *binge*. "Bingeing and purging" conjures up all kinds of images, mostly unpleasant. Enough said on that point.

There is a positive connotation to the word *purge* as well. It's the process of purification, decontamination, cleaning out, removing waste. It's a helpful and healthful exercise for doing away with gunk and junk.

When I reminded Molly of our "purge day," I was getting psyched up for the monumental task of cleaning out our basement, the cavernous space where all our extra stuff and worn-out items end up. Once or twice a year we finally get fed up with the accumulated mess and call for a purge. Never fun, but always necessary—and a relief when it's over. We get rid of half-read books, obsolete files, old toys, broken exercise equipment, and bags of hand-me-down clothes. Where did all this stuff come from anyway? At the end of the day, we've got boxes, bags, and bins ready for the local mission or recycling center or dump. Finally, we stand in a miraculously clean, clutter-free, and suddenly spacious basement, amazed that something so dirty and messy a few hours before could now feel so inviting and enjoyable.

A purging process is not only helpful for our actual basement (or garage, guest room, or storage unit). Each of us has an internal space where our emotional and spiritual junk piles up. Our heart is like a basement holding a trove of both treasures and trash, beloved prizes and broken pieces. It's where we hide all that stuff we want to ignore, stuff we don't want houseguests to notice, stuff that nags at us and weighs us down.

God invites us to bring all the treasures we have to Him and celebrate them, but also to come to Him ready to purge. We can get rid of all the junk in our lives that serves as a roadblock between ourselves and God. We can clear out all the debris and detritus we trip over on our way to an honest relationship with Him.

A big part of this involves the confession of sin. In the last chapter we talked about the importance of acknowledging our sin and seeking forgiveness for it. While sin molders in our basement, it stinks and rots and attracts flies. Confession is our way of admitting that our garbage exists, accepting responsibility for bringing it into the house, and asking God to take it to the incinerator, to be burned in His purifying fire. Gone forever.

There's another aspect to the purging process. Often it's our heartaches and hurts that need to be brought up out of the basement. Our wounds can be like rubble that needs to be cleaned up so we can move forward in our relationship with God. Life is full of things that can and do hurt us. The pain we bring on ourselves is hard enough to endure; it can be even more intense when someone else gives us a wound we don't deserve.

King David, who wrote most of the Psalms, tells us what to do: "Trust in him at all times, O people; pour out your heart before him; God is a refuge for us" (Psalm 62:8). One thing God does well is listen, and He invites us to tell Him all our troubles. Some people feel such profound shame and guilt that they don't want to open the basement door to their hearts, let alone allow God to look at what's down there. Some people are hesitant to express their anger to God, fearing lightning bolts from heaven.

Still, above all, God desires a *relationship* with His children, and a genuine relationship is impossible without honest communication. The Bible itself provides many examples of believers who vented, protested, and sobbed before God. The Psalms are filled with heartfelt and anguished pleas. The book of Jeremiah shows the "weeping prophet" regularly spilling his guts to God. Jesus Himself prayed, "My God, my God, why have you forsaken me?" (Matthew 27:46). By opening our heart to God, we allow Him to bring healing and wholeness.

In fact, the primary purpose of purging is transformation. Sure, it feels good just to express ourselves and let our feelings flow out. That's cathartic and curative in itself. But most of all, the process of purging says to God, "I'm clearing space in my heart and soul so You can have room to remodel and redecorate as You see fit." The process allows change to happen at the deepest levels.

How can we go about purging our sin and pain? Consider the following guideposts.

OWN UP TO IT

When I've got the big mess to clean up in my basement, my first impulse is to turn off the light, close the door, and pretend it's not there. I've even made false walls out of bedsheets to hide sections of my messy basement. Out of sight, out of mind.

Well, not really. In the back of my mind, I know it's there, needing attention and intervention. Avoiding the problem doesn't make it go away. When it comes to our own mistakes and failings, it's all too easy to rationalize or scapegoat. We blame and finger-point, refusing to accept responsibility. Our society has elevated blame-shifting to an art form, as people justify their own bad behavior by focusing on someone else's guilt.

Jesus used a compelling metaphor when talking about personal accountability. "Why do you see the speck that is in your brother's eye, but do not notice the log that is in your own eye? Or how can you say to your brother, 'Let me take the speck out of your eye,' when there is the log in your own eye. You hypocrite, first take the log out of your own eye, and then you will see clearly to take the speck out of your brother's eye" (Matthew 7:3–5). The purging process begins by taking ownership for what we've done.

The same goes for pain we feel, which might or might not have been caused by something we did. Pretending that pain doesn't exist doesn't mean it's not there. Lots of people cram their hurts in a box, wrap it tightly with duct tape, and shove it to the farthest corner of the basement. I talk all the time with people who rationalize or minimize bad things that have happened to them. People say "I'm fine" so often they come to believe it themselves, though they're far from being *fine*. Before you can experience the waste removal of God's forgiveness or healing touch, you must acknowledge the gravity of your situation and the pain it's causing. You have to face the truth and sift through all of the resulting heartaches.

LOOK SQUARELY AT THE SITUATION

If you're like me, you can find a thousand excuses for putting off something you don't want to do. I can walk a mile around a mess I don't want to clean up. I can make twenty unimportant phone calls until I finally work up the courage to make that one really important and difficult call.

Sounds kind of like the way we interact with—or avoid interacting with—God. We sometimes spend lots of time talking to Him about everything except the things we should really be telling Him. I remember in high school literature class reading Mark Twain's *The Adventures of Huckleberry Finn*. At one point, Huck finds himself in a moral quandary. He says, "I made up my mind to pray, and see if I couldn't try to quit being the kind of a boy I was and be better. So I kneeled down. But the words wouldn't come. . . . It warn't no use to try and hide it from Him. . . . Deep down in me I knowed it was a lie, and He knowed it. You can't pray a lie—I found that out."

Well said, Huck. When we're struggling with sin or pain, we ought to tell it like it is. As I said previously, God already knows everything about us and sees what we'd like to hide. He knows you messed up. He knows your friend betrayed you. He knows you're heartbroken over your parents' divorce. He knows you've been living a lie. Why not be honest about how angry or afraid you are?

If you want God to help remove all the junk cluttering up your heart and mind, tell Him exactly what's going on with you. When you purge, lay it out there. Look squarely at what's in your heart and talk about it openly. Cleansing begins the moment you give yourself the freedom to be who you are—with all the pain and problems, failures and fiascos.

LOOK TO THE EXAMPLES IN THE BIBLE

When it comes to spiritual and emotional purging, we also have an endless supply of help in the pages of the Bible. More than two-thirds of the Psalms are *laments*, in which the writer pours out his thoughts and feelings to God. If you're unsure how to go about it, you might follow the typical five-part pattern of these psalms.

Introductory call to God. The psalmist respectfully calls upon God to listen and respond, with words such as "Have mercy on me, O God, according to your steadfast love" (51:1). Or "Listen to my prayer, O God, do not ignore my plea; hear me and answer me" (55:1–2 NIV).

Lament—expression of pain or confession. The psalmist then passionately communicates his distress or problem. Describing his situation in detail, he says what his enemies have done, what challenges he's facing, or what consequences sin has brought about.

Declaration of trust. Switching from the complaint or confession, the psalmist states his confidence in God to come through.

Request. The psalmist then asks for what he wants God to do—for instance, to intervene in some practical way, provide strength to persevere, or grant forgiveness for wrongdoing.

Thanks and praise. The conclusion is the expression of gratitude that God has listened and will answer according to His will. It also includes praises for God's qualities, such as faithfulness, compassion, and justice.

Some people find it helpful to follow this structure. Others prefer to read specific psalms as prayers, personalizing them as much as possible. For starters, read Psalm 34, a plea for protection; Psalm 51, a cry of confession of sin; or Psalm 73, an appeal for God's justice.

GRIEVE AND SAY GOOD-BYE

There comes a point when you just need to bend down, pick up the box of junk, let out a groan, and haul it away. You've got to make a decision to get rid of things, and sometimes it's hard to let go.

As with the physical things we accumulate, we all have attachments to emotional and spiritual things that need to be released and relinquished. These might be bad habits, misguided beliefs, old hurts, or stubborn sins. To experience freedom, we need to do the hard work of prying destructive attitudes and actions from our lives. All of our bitter and resentful emotions need to be uprooted.

To overcome deep wounds, we may need the help of a counselor or pastor who can provide a safe environment to process pain. To overcome persistent sins or tough habits, we may need an accountability group or a mentor to provide encouragement and accountability. To overcome any kind of issue, we'll certainly need to summon up our self-discipline, intentionality, and focus.

Mostly what we need is God's Spirit to move in the deepest recesses of our lives. You've probably heard the term "filled with the Spirit." This biblical phrase simply means to be *controlled and empowered by* the Holy Spirit within you. If you are a Christian, the Holy Spirit lives within you and does not leave you. If you are a "Spirit-filled Christian," the Holy Spirit is in charge of your life. You are granting Him control to teach, guide, comfort, and empower your spiritual journey. And that is when purging becomes transformational in our lives.

ENJOY THE CLEAN, OPEN SPACE

Emptying a cluttered, messy area can be arduous and exhausting. Therefore, don't forget to celebrate when the job is done. Stand back, take a deep breath, look around, and let out a victory yell!

David said, "I will exalt you, Lord, for you lifted me out of the depths. . . . You turned my wailing into dancing" (Psalm 30:1, 11 NIV). When we pour out our sins before God, asking for His grace and mercy, we have cause for celebration. Why? Because we have

God's assurance of forgiveness (see 1 John 1:9). We can delight in the promise of His Word. Because of Jesus' death and resurrection and our acceptance of Him, we are assured of God's compassionate grace as His children. We can rejoice in His love and come to Him in full honesty.

What's gained when we purge before God is freedom—freedom from the sins that hold us back, freedom from the pain that weighs us down. I love the way author Brennan Manning puts it: "Blessed are you if your laughter means that you have let go in reckless confidence all that shackles you to yesterday, imprisons you in your small self today, and frightens you with the uncertainty of tomorrow. Blessed are you who laugh, because you are free!" *

Is it time to clean out your basement? If you've got junk and clutter down there, resist the urge to seal off the door and pretend it's not there. Throw open the door, and set about purging. So that change can happen. So that God has more room in your heart to refurbish, restore, and remodel.

* Brennan Manning, *Reflections for Ragamuffins* (San Francisco: HarperSanFrancisco, 1998), 96.

CHAPTER 14

RADICAL INTEGRITY

THE PRICE—AND REWARD—OF LIVING HONESTLY
IN A DISHONEST WORLD

It is safe to say that sitting alone at the bottom of a dry well, where your own brothers have tossed you and left you to who-knows-what fate, would present a perfect opportunity to rethink your life. Choking on dust, with no way out and only spiders for company, would make anyone ask: What in the world went wrong?

I imagine that very question was going through Joseph's mind as he gazed upward at the shrunken disc of blue sky above him—possibly the last thing he would ever see in this life. How had he come to this? The longer he thought about it, the clearer the answer became: He'd simply been honest—some might say a little *too* honest. After all, it is possible to tell the truth at the wrong time, with no sensitivity to the feelings of others.

Nevertheless, Joseph had told his parents and brothers about a pair of dreams he'd had that cast all of them in a less-than-desirable role, at least from their point of view. In the first, Joseph and

143

his brothers were harvesting sheaves of grain. Suddenly his sheave rose up, and all the others bowed down to it. In a second dream, he was surrounded by the sun and moon and eleven stars—representing his father and mother and each of his brothers—and, again, all bowed before him.

Joseph's brothers already resented him bitterly because their father doted on him and seemed to love him the most. This time, the pretentious little punk had gone too far, actually suggesting it was his *destiny* to rule over them and command their obedience one day. Even Jacob, his father, scolded him for his adolescent arrogance.

Still, as the sunlight faded and nighttime shadows deepened in the well, Joseph may have reminded himself he'd done no more than tell the truth. God had given him a gift, the ability to see the hidden meaning in dreams. Could it really be so wrong to share it with others? His brothers thought so. At the first good opportunity, they said, "Come now, let us kill him and throw him into one of the pits. Then we will say that a fierce animal has devoured him, and we will see what will become of his dreams" (Genesis 37:20).

Surely it would have ended in death if Reuben hadn't convinced them to drop their little brother into a dry well instead, hoping to rescue the boy from murder and bring him safely home to their father. Later, while they were eating, Judah thought up a brilliant plan to get rid of Joseph for good *and* turn a tidy profit in the process: Why not sell him to slave traders bound for Egypt? They could still tell Jacob his youngest boy had been mauled by a wild animal, but they'd have no real blood on their hands. The co-conspirators eagerly agreed, and before Rueben could intervene again, Joseph was in Ishmaelite shackles on his way across the desert to a whole new life.

Now if anyone had a good reason to conclude that too much honesty is bad for you, it was Joseph. Who could blame him if he had decided to clam up and keep his head down for the rest of his life? He could have grown bitter and angry at a world that could be so cruel, and at God. But that's not what happened. In fact, it wasn't long before he was at it again, telling the truth and getting into trouble for it.

TRUTH—OR DARE TO DISPLEASE GOD

In Egypt, Joseph was sold to Potiphar, the captain of Pharaoh's guard. Right away the man could see there was something special about his new servant; everything the strange Hebrew did succeeded because "the Lord was with him." In no time, Potiphar put Joseph in charge of his entire household, "and because of him he had no concern about anything but the food he ate." All was well.

Sort of. Potiphar was married to a lustful woman who liked the new slave as much as her husband did, but for entirely different reasons. Joseph was "handsome in form and appearance," and, as the master's wife, she commanded him to sleep with her. Being an honest man—above all in his relationship with God—Joseph refused. He listed all the ways in which her husband had been good to him and deserved his loyalty. He said, "How then can I do this great wickedness and sin against God?"

Let's be frank: A less honest man might not risk the severe consequences of getting caught sleeping with his master's wife, even if she ordered him to. But he'd probably do all he could to sweet-talk and keep her happy. Maybe even play along for a while and cross a boundary here and there, just to keep the peace. Better to be a little bad, and alive, than honest and dead, right?

Not our man Joseph. He told the truth and called her proposal what it was: "great wickedness" and "sin against God." He practically pleaded with her to reconsider. His integrity, *radical* honesty and openness before God, demanded nothing less.

It is quite possible seventeenth-century poet William Congreve had Potiphar's wife in mind when he wrote, "Hell hath no fury like a woman scorned." Having had enough of Joseph's "integrity," and perhaps fearing he would eventually tell her husband what she was up to, Potiphar's wife lied and accused Joseph of making advances toward *her*. Like his brothers had done, she figured out how to get rid of his uncomfortable honesty by getting rid of *him*. Before the sun set, Joseph lost everything (again) and was back in shackles, this time locked away in an Egyptian prison with little hope of release.

RAGS TO RICHES

Surely *now*, after two consecutive slaps in the face, you'd think Joseph would swear off honesty forever, giving up and concluding his precious integrity had brought him nothing but heartache and loss. But Joseph knew better. It says repeatedly in his story that "he trusted God," even in light of the unfavorable circumstances. He accepted that living honestly before God in a thoroughly dishonest world can be costly at time*s*. *Very* costly, in fact. It has the power to provoke the animosity of those who'd rather remain hidden in the shadow of sin than submit to the naked vulnerability of openness with God.

More importantly, Joseph knew a fact we too must grasp if we are going to overcome our fears and fully commit to honesty before God: *The high cost of radical integrity in the world is insignificant compared to the benefit of God's blessing when we are transparent with Him.* Whatever price we pay, we get back much, much more in unhindered intimacy with God and access to His transformative power in our daily lives. As Paul wrote, "I consider that the sufferings of this present time are not worth comparing with the glory that is to be revealed to us" (Romans 8:18).

That's why Joseph rose to the top everywhere he went: God's glorious blessing. Pleased with him, God lifted Joseph above his suffering and gave him a truly abundant life. Don't believe it? Read to the end of the story.

While still in prison, and through a series of providential events, Joseph correctly interpreted the dreams of Pharaoh himself and was promoted to the *very* top. He became prime minister over all Egypt. The pharaoh said to him, "Without your consent no one shall lift up hand or foot in all the land of Egypt" (Genesis 41:44).

Talk about your rags to riches story! And yet God *still* wasn't finished affirming His approval and affection for Joseph. The drama now comes full circle, back to where it started. Years later, severe famine in their own country forced Joseph's brothers to come to Egypt for help and to bow down before Joseph, whom they no longer even recognized. He alone had the authority to save them or send them away hungry, just as his dreams had foretold so long ago. Once more, he chose to honor God and act with integrity. He set aside his natural desire for revenge. He forgave his brothers and saved his people, sharing with them the bounty he'd laid up in Egypt.

WORTH THE PRICE

There is no way around it: Joseph's honesty and openness with God, which led him to a life of radical integrity in his relationships with others—cost Joseph dearly. For a time he lost his father and mother and his inheritance as their son. He lost the freedom to do as he pleased, becoming a slave and then a prisoner, forgotten and despised. Every step of the way he risked the dangerous disapproval of those who were threatened by his honesty.

But God's honesty plan never stops there. Alongside all he suffered, Joseph also enjoyed God's priceless fellowship and blessing. Everything he did succeeded, though not always in the way he expected.

Here's the bottom line for us in our quest for greater honesty with God and others: We may not wind up in chains or face the threat of death, as Joseph did, but we will pay *something* for living with radical integrity, guaranteed. It is inevitable in a world still bound by the shame of sin and the need to run and hide from truth, wherever it appears. There is no point in pretending it isn't so.

I will never forget the moment a few years ago when I was tempted to throw away my integrity for the sake of saving a friendship. To make a long story short, I had grown very close with my boss who was also the associate pastor of the church where I served. We had many great moments together over long lunches or afternoon coffee breaks. He taught me some of the greatest church leadership lessons I've ever learned.

As our friendship grew, I started to see actions he took within the church that didn't seem right. Extended times away from the church and excessive spending on the church card had become the norm. But his activities were inconspicuous enough that even I found myself creating excuses for his behavior.

After a few weeks of sleepless nights and a lot of internal turmoil, I decided something had to be done. He was messing with the bride of Christ and I knew the groom, Christ Himself, was not happy.

Although I knew it would probably kill our friendship, I had to turn him in. My attempts to directly confront him only led to more lies. I was left with no choice but to tell the lead pastor and the board. With the help of a faithful friend, who also risked his reputation, we brought forth the facts. This led to an immediate and forced resignation. As my friend walked down the hall after being asked to leave his position, I remember grieving the loss of friendship so deeply that I could physically feel it. Sadly, we have not talked since, at his request.

Through that situation and others, I have learned that to live a life like Joseph will require (1) total trust in God, believing that He is always in control of the outcome; (2) openness with God and others about the areas of failure in our life; and (3) commitment to never compromise God's standard, no matter the cost.

So evaluate your situation. What are the small areas where Satan can get a foothold in your life? Where has the Enemy convinced you that a little lie won't hurt anyone, including yourself or God? Where are you cutting corners because you think no one really cares? Radical integrity is not only costly, but it is inclusive of every area of our life. A stolen stapler, some extramarital flirtation, or unflattering gossip are all equally fractures to our honesty in God's eyes. As I have come to realize, living with the uprightness of Joseph is not without its challenges.

Nevertheless, by the time you have reaped the limitless rewards of unguarded intimacy with God and the blessings that always follow, you will barely remember what it cost you to get there. Like Joseph, for the sake of your Lord, you'd do it all over again.

CHAPTER 15

THE PRIZE OF PURPOSE

HOW HONESTY WITH GOD CAN SETTLE THE QUESTION OF WHAT YOU ARE MEANT TO DO IN LIFE

I didn't want to be a pastor.

No, that's not entirely accurate—I *really* didn't want to be a pastor. I had been involved in ministry in one way or another since I was a kid. I'd spoken to thousands of young people, helped launch and support campus ministries, including one at Columbine High School prior to the tragic shootings there, and started a radio show in Chicago called *Honest to God.*

But I *knew* that being a pastor, taking a leadership role in the spiritual lives of people in a particular congregation, was not my *purpose.* For years it would have been hard for you to discern exactly what I did think my purpose might be. I worked as a magician, lawn mower, meat packager, coffee shop barista, ice hockey scorekeeper, donut maker, busboy, manager of shopping mall Santa and Easter Bunny stands, and restaurant waiter. Not much of a pattern there. Like most young people I was attempting to find out what *I* wanted to do with my life, so that I could let God in on it and receive His blessing.

Finally it came to me: I wanted to own a coffee shop. I love coffee, and I love the idea of providing a place where people can come together and visit, or simply sit and enjoy a few moments away from the frenetic bustle of life outside. I explained to God how my coffee shop would be a kind of ministry too, dedicated to Him and to the goal of loving people one at a time, in the midst of their chaotic lives. I promised to give away piles of money once coffee had made me wealthy. I envisioned impromptu Bible studies around the tables and scores of people who would remember the shop and say, "That's where I met the Lord."

I got busy raising money to make this dream come true. I needed $80,000 and found the first $50,000 right away—a sure sign of God's favor, I thought. Then, as if suddenly stuck in a maze of dead ends, I couldn't find another dollar of start-up capital. My plans came to a screeching halt. At this point, deep down, I knew that God had other ideas for me, but I did my best to ignore that fact. I had some very "honest" conversations with the Lord that always ended the same: *"Please, give me the rest of the money and I promise You will be glorified through this coffee shop."*

But I was forgetting something vitally important about an open and honest relationship with God: It's a two-way street. In other words, honesty is about *listening* to God as much as speaking our minds to Him. I had been telling God what I thought I wanted to do with my life, but hadn't yet asked what He wanted.

TWO PATHS

Still convinced that coffee was my future, I reluctantly accepted a friend's invitation to attend a pastors' conference with him. As the date drew closer, I tried to find an excuse to cancel, but the trip was already paid for, so backing out would have been awkward. I searched for someone to take my place and came up empty. Finally, I resigned myself to go—for my friend's sake. The truth is, I didn't want to be anywhere near pastors. They *annoyed* me.

About the time funds dried up for my coffee shop venture, and before I was hauled off to the pastors' powwow against my will, I received an unexpected invitation from Creekside Church in Denver to become a candidate for the position of teaching pastor. I politely told them I didn't want to be a pastor and, for good measure, sent a list of stringent conditions that would have to be met if I ever, ever were to even *consider* such a thing. It must have made the elders smile to receive a response that said, "No way! But here's how to get me to change my mind." They might have recalled a bit of Shakespeare: "He doth protest too much, methinks!" That's often how it is when we are running from an uncomfortable choice.

But notice an important detail: I still did not get honest with God and say, "Is this what *You* want me to do?"

Off I went to the conference like a kid being dragged from the playground to go to a Wednesday night prayer meeting. One of the few sessions I actually attended was led by a pastor from Texas named Matt Chandler. The bottom line is this: His story was eerily similar to mine. He'd avoided pastoral ministry with all his might. He'd received an invitation to interview for the pastor position of a small Texas church. He gave them a list of conditions he felt sure would send them running the other way. He told his wife with relief that he'd "dodged that bullet!"

In the end, the congregation agreed to his terms and offered him the job.

Years later, as he told his story at the conference, he implied that when he finally got around to asking God what *He* wanted, everything became clear. In spite of his reluctance, Chandler took the position and instantly *knew* he had stepped smack into the center of God's purpose for him.

As I listened, I knew I had run out of wiggle room. For all my talk about honesty with God—hours on the radio and in dozens of blogged articles—I had failed to see the most important element of openness and transparency with Him: Surrender to His will in all things. That night I did what I should have done from the beginning—I let God have His say. His answer was no big surprise.

The next morning I got up, grabbed my computer, and set out for the hotel lobby, intending to send the resume Creekside had requested. Not that all my reservations had vanished—far from it! But I could no longer pretend I was in charge of the decision. I would take the step right in front of me and go from there.

Who do you suppose was waiting at the elevator when I arrived to head down? Matt Chandler, on his way to the airport for an early flight.

"What are you doing up at the crack of dawn?" he asked.

Shaking my head at God's penchant for using coincidence to underline His leadings, I told him the whole story. The conversation ended when he simply said, "Yeah, you need to pursue that." And I remember the moment being much more than one man giving advice to another. It was as if God Himself were saying to me, *Josh, just trust Me. I have a plan for you and it's much greater than the plan you have for yourself.*

I sent the resume and later received an offer to become pastor of the Creekside Church congregation by a unanimous vote. During this time, my wife became pregnant with our firstborn son whom we named "Chandler" as a way of remembering God's faithfulness to us even when we are stubborn in our unfaithfulness toward Him.

Upon beginning leadership at Creekside, I accepted that pastoring was God's purpose for me, without question. Oh, I still sit in coffee shops and wonder what might have been. I still struggle with some of the unique challenges of being a pastor. But each day I get out of bed knowing I am exactly where God wants me, doing precisely what He has called me to do. No more guessing games about whether my life is on the right track. Honesty led me directly to my God-given *purpose*.

BE WHO GOD WANTS YOU TO BE

Serving coffee is an excellent profession and a worthy goal. So is owning a business, or learning a trade, or going to college, or raising children. Just about anything can be God's purpose for your life. But, as believers, we must accept the truth embedded in that sentence—that it is *God's* purpose for us that matters. Deep openness and honesty with Him—the willingness to ask what He desires and then follow where He leads—is the only way to separate His voice from the deafening din of competing messages we receive every day about how to choose what's right for us.

The world's criteria for true success are obvious and predictable—the tired trio of power, fortune, and fame. Who knows, God's plan for you may include some or all of those things. Yet, even then, you will only know for sure you are in the center of God's will by honestly seeking what He desires for you. Nothing else will ever come close to giving you a meaningful and fulfilling life.

Now don't get me wrong—just because we find God's purpose for us doesn't mean that every day will be rainbows and butterflies. Bad days are bound to come. Discouragement will dog us without ceasing in certain seasons of our life. Yet, when our purpose has come out of honest conversations with and complete submission to God, we will know the route we need to take to return to the peace of His presence.

That was the problem with the prophet Jonah. He only had

honest conversations with God when things weren't going according to *his* plan. God had given him a grand call to preach to his enemy, the brutal Assyrians of Nineveh. A simple, open conversation with God could have exposed Jonah's heart to God and allowed for Jonah's mind-set to be changed from the onset. But instead he decided to run and hide. It wasn't until he was in the belly of a fish that he decided to open his heart and confess how far he had gotten away from total surrender to God.

By God's great mercy he was saved, once from the storm, and again from dying inside the fish. Now on dry land, God aimed his feet down the path of purpose he had been created for. He went, but reluctantly. He delivered his message and then ran. He went to the top of the highest hill he could find to watch what he hoped would be the wrath of God poured out on his enemy—just the way he thought it should be.

To his great surprise, and much to his dismay, God saved the people of Nineveh. Jonah had to be thinking the whole time, *Are you kidding me! This is not what I had in mind!* In fact the Bible even tells us that "It displeased Jonah exceedingly, and he was angry" (Jonah 4:1).

Then one of the most honest dialogues in Scripture between God and man unfolds.

Jonah said, "O Lord, is not this what I said when I was yet in my country? That is why I made haste to flee to Tarshish; for I knew that you are a gracious God and merciful, slow to anger and abounding in steadfast love, and relenting from disaster. Therefore now, O Lord, please take my life from me, for it is better for me to die than to live" (Jonah 4:2–3).

In other words, Jonah knew good and well that God was merciful and that God would use him as a catalyst to display that mercy. Jonah didn't want anything to do with that purpose, or God's mercy on the Assyrians—even though God's mercy was the very thing that had saved Jonah up to that point. Jonah thought death was a better option than to accept the reality of God's purpose for him.

In response to Jonah's anger, God gently rebuked him by asking, "Do you do well to be angry?"

With that honest and searching question, Jonah gave no reply but chose to pout.

We are guilty of the same response. When we don't get the status, opportunities, or outcomes we think we should have, we give God a piece of our mind. Sometimes this looks like nothing more than an angry teenager stomping up the stairs and out of the presence of his father. Honesty with God isn't sharing with Him where we think we've been shortchanged and then giving Him the silent treatment. True honesty with God encounters God with open palms, looking to Him to reveal and guide us through His purpose for our lives.

As we begin to close this journey together on the path to honesty, let me pause on the hills of Nineveh in the account of Jonah and ask you, Have you openly relinquished your small dreams to God's greater glory? Or are you allowing your dissatisfaction with where you are to be like that of Jonah, wishing for a different set of circumstances because you hate where God has you? Don't let your temporary desires be the hindrance to a life of surrender to God. Open up, listen to Him, and see for yourself that true surrender will take you deeper and further with God than you ever dreamed.

HONESTY IS A MEANS TO TRANSFORMATION

WHEN YOU ARE TRULY HONEST WITH GOD, IT IS IMPOSSIBLE TO STAY THE SAME

Suppose for a moment that we will all have jobs in heaven. Imagine that each one of us will uphold a divine occupation in which we will function for the rest of eternity. If this is true, I know exactly what position I will apply for upon my arrival.

THE CROWN HANDLER

I want to stand as close to Jesus as possible. The mere benefit of being in His presence would be the honor of the job of Crown Handler. I am sure my employment in this position would never become routine because I would be able to watch all the new arrivals enter into the kingdom of God. I want to see the looks on the faces of those who see Jesus for the first time. I want to be there, looking right over Christ's shoulder, when *you* see Jesus face-to-face. I imagine your expression will light up brighter than a bride at the end of the aisle on her wedding day. I am sure I will cry as I watch the tears well up in your eyes because of the joy rising inside you. As you move closer to

Jesus, I can imagine Him saying with excitement, "At last, My child, welcome home!"

After you share the most significant embrace you've ever experienced, I envision Christ turning and asking for the crown crafted just for you. I see myself taking it out of the box and marveling at its beauty, a mere symbol of the great inheritance given to you because of your faith in Christ and your obedience to Him. I would hand it to Jesus and watch Him place it on your head. Your eyes would shimmer with excitement as you tried to comprehend blessing on top of blessing. Then you would fall straight to your knees. There you would bow and worship the very person who has been the greatest object of your affection. Without hesitation you would slip the crown off of your head and place it at the feet of Christ, for you know there is no better place for it. With that, you might well hear Him say, "Well done, good and faithful servant. Enter into the joy of your master" (Matthew 25:21, 23).

The Master's joy consists of two main ingredients: knowing and being known. To be welcomed into this kind of joy is to be invited to know God intimately. It is also *to be known* completely—raw, unhindered, accepted, and forgiven. The pinnacle of all honesty with God comes when we find great joy in knowing God and being known by Him. But this type of joy does not commence in heaven; it is a continuation of what you can experience in this life. If we are living honest to God while we are here on earth, our communion with Him in heaven will merely be a fuller sense of His presence, a natural extension of intimacy.

HERE AND THERE

We don't have to wait for heaven to have unhindered communion with Christ—we can have that now! Scripture portrays this time and again by showing us instances of gut-wrenching honesty that result in life-altering intimacy with God.

One of the most "honest-to-God" psalms was written by Asaph, a young temple worship leader grappling with the reasons why he should remain righteous (see Psalm 73). Not only was he talented, but he was also highly esteemed by King David and the temple goers. Yet, as he observed how evil people seemed to prosper, he felt jealous, and wrote about the experience in this psalm. He candidly made some bold statements like:

> "I was envious of the arrogant."
> "All in vain have I kept my heart clean and washed my hands in innocence."
> "For all the day long I have been stricken and rebuked every morning."

Yet, after a bit of venting about how he felt, seventeen verses in, Asaph's honesty was the very tool God used to change him completely. With all his feelings now out on the table, He entered the sanctuary of God and *everything changed*. He now saw God as He really was (vv. 1, 24–26), discerned the wrathful end of the wicked (vv. 18–20), and acknowledged that he was in a bad place (vv. 2, 21–22). Asaph's honesty was not an end in itself, but a means to true transformation. His closing words were a confession of trust and change: "But for me it is good to be near God; I have made the Lord God my refuge" (v. 28). I think it is safe to say that Asaph was able to at least taste the Master's joy this side of heaven.

AN HONEST-TO-GOD LIFE

As we close this journey together, my prayer for you is that your vulnerability with God will lead you to greater intimacy with Him. Dispel an artificial Christianity that is only superficial by applying the lessons from the Bible we have learned in this book:

- *Stop hiding.* Because of our sin, we cower from God like Adam and Eve did in the garden. We hide in the hedges of our shame, fear, guilt, and insecurities. Come out of hiding and simply say, "Here I am," allowing His righteousness to cover you completely.

• *Resign from image management.* We have made a profession of pretending to be someone we are not. We manage our image before God, others, and even ourselves. Sometimes even unknowingly, we care far more about tending to our outward appearance and what others perceive of us rather than what lies soul deep. Remember, Christ didn't die for your image, He came to save your soul. Remove the facade and lay your life bare for the sake of change.

• *See God as He really is.* Our disease of dishonesty stems from a small (and wrong) view of God. Until we see God as He really is, we never will see ourselves for who we really are. By the grace of God through the gospel of Christ, we can be forgiven from our past and the scales can be removed from our eyes. With the help of the Holy Spirit, embrace a biblical view of God.

• *Engage in God's Honesty Plan.* An honest encounter with God will never leave you the same. When you drop your guard, embrace the gospel of grace, and begin being honest, you will find the freedom you have been longing for. You will be able to purge the past, have integrity in the present, and live with excitement for God's purposes for you in the future.

As you strive for honesty, remember you are not alone. People like Moses, Abraham, Joseph, Joshua, Esther, Asaph, David, Jeremiah, Isaiah, Hosea, and many others have dared to live unhindered lives of dedication to their Lord. Follow their examples and hold up your life before God, allowing His light to reveal where you need Him the most. The Old Testament principle of being completely honest with God is impossible without the New Testament application of Christ's redemption. A person who has Christ at the center of their existence will experience fellowship with God, and find they have nothing to hide.

ACKNOWLEDGEMENTS

I am grateful to be surrounded by the wonderful men and women who have made this book possible. God receives the glory for this project, but these are the instruments God used to accomplish His purposes. I would like to thank the following:

My Lord and Savior, Jesus Christ for allowing me to know God and be known by Him completely.

Keith Wall for modeling the high calling to write and edit with excellence.

Alan Wartes for bringing a deep authenticity to the pages of this book.

Stephanie Roth for your faithfulness to speak truth, love the gospel, and value words.

Dr. Schmutzer for teaching me to love the God of the Bible without reservation.

Roger Basick for being a faithful friend, producer, and partner in *Honest to God Radio*.

Jenni Burke and Don Jacobson for believing in me and stewarding my calling to write.

Penny Whipps for always encouraging me to write even when I wanted to give up.

Randall Payleitner for taking the risk to partner with me and call a generation to God.

Chris Reese for all the "good calls" and great editing to make the words dance.

My son, Chandler, for helping relieve the daily weight of ministry with a simple smile.

My dad for being my companion, comrade, and mentor every day of my life.

My mom for being the endless source of God's love and compassion I always need.

My siblings, Jake, Janae, Joy, and Micah, for cheering me on in all my crazy endeavors.

My Gold relatives for loving me endlessly.

Ken Murphy for countless hours of mentoring to help me love the gospel more.

Mike Romberger for supporting me while I wrote and pastored through some of my darkest hours.

David Jones for helping me love God and steward His Word wisely.

Creekside Bible Church for trusting me to be their pastor and inviting me into their lives.

UNFRIEND YOURSELF

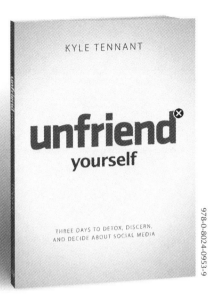

KYLE TENNANT

unfriendⓧ
yourself

THREE DAYS TO DETOX, DISCERN,
AND DECIDE ABOUT SOCIAL MEDIA

978-0-8024-0953-9

We are all connected. To each other, to our devices, to our networks, to everything ... The world of social media has turned the rest of our worlds upside down. Can you disconnect for three days to assess the situation in your own life? This short book is split into three sections to help you DETOX, DISCERN, and DECIDE what role Facebook, Twitter, Google+, and all the rest can and should have in your life. *Unfriend Yourself* will help you think critically, biblically, and practically from a Christian perspective about the merits and ramifications of our social media culture. Don't worry, the world can wait; your friends won't even know you're gone—seriously, there are over half a billion of them out there. I doubt you'll be missed.

MOODY
Publishers™

*From the Word **to** Life*

MoodyPublishers.com

HOW TO RUIN YOUR LIFE BY 30

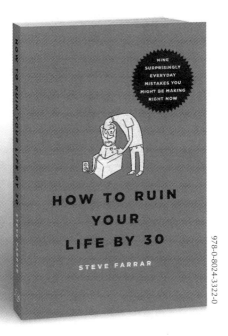

Everyone has an internal alarm clock that goes off when they're about to make a bad decision. Some men and women spend their 20s hitting the snooze button. Steve Farrar gives them the wake-up call that they can't escape, to help them avoid the life-shattering consequences of foolish choices. Upon speaking at Biola University, Steve Farrar made an instant connection with the students, generating tremendous response. This book springs out of their burning questions and struggles. It helps young men and women fix their mistakes before they make them, but it also can help readers recover from poor choices before it's too late.

MOODY
Publishers™

From the Word to Life

MoodyPublishers.com

THE ROAD TRIP THAT CHANGED THE WORLD

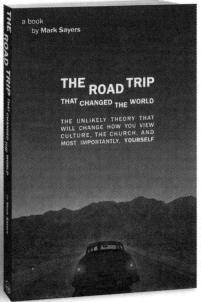

a book
by **Mark Sayers**

THE ROAD TRIP
THAT CHANGED THE WORLD

THE UNLIKELY THEORY THAT
WILL CHANGE HOW YOU VIEW
CULTURE, THE CHURCH, AND
MOST IMPORTANTLY, YOURSELF

978-0-8024-0931-7

Sixty years ago a goatee beard would have gotten you beat up in a lot
of places. Chin fuzz was the symbol of the Beats or Beatniks, a mid-
century, marginal group who pioneered a new kind of lifestyle that
was hedonistic, experiential, and individualistic. Their contradictory
approach to spirituality combined a search for God with a search for
"kicks." In 1947, these Beatnik heroes set out on a road trip across
America re-writing the "life-script" of all future generations. They
modeled a new approach to faith: desiring Christ, while still pursuing
a laundry list of vices. Yet this dream would turn into a nightmare, and
the open road would lead back to an ancient, half-forgotten path. It
was a path that began with a single step of faith as a pilgrim named
Abraham stepped away from a cynical culture. A path of devotion that
led to a cross on Golgotha.

MOODY
Publishers™

*From the Word **to Life***

MoodyPublishers.com